Brave New Schools:

How Computers Can Change Education

Glenn M. Kleiman

A Reston Computer Group Book
Reston Publishing Company, Inc.
Reston, Virginia
A Prentice-Hall Company

Bank Street Writer™ (home version) is a trademark of Broderbund Software, Inc., San Rafael, CA 94901

Bank Street Writer™ (school version) is a trademark of Scholastic, Inc. Jefferson City, MO 65102

Dialog℠ is a service mark of DIALOG Information Services, Palo Alto, CA 94304

MasterType™ is a trademark of Lightning Software, Palo Alto, CA 94306

Maxit is copyrighted (1981) by The Code Works, *Cursor Magazine*, Goleta, CA 93116

Meteor Multiplication™ is a trademark of Developmental Learning Materials, Allen, TX 75002

Oregon Trail is part of *Elementary Volume 6*, copyrighted by the Minnesota Educational Computing Consortium (MECC), St. Paul, MN 55113

Pinball Construction Set™ is a trademark of Electronic Arts, San Mateo, CA 94403

The Source℠ is a service mark of Source Telecomputing Corporation, McLean, VA 22102, a subsidiary of the Reader's Digest Association

VersaBraille™ is a trademark of Telesensory Systems, Inc., Palo Alto, CA 94304

Library of Congress Cataloging in Publication Data

Kleiman, Glenn M.
  Brave new schools.

  "A Reston computer group book."
  Includes bibliographical references and index.
  1. Computer-assisted instruction. I. Title.
LB10285.K547   1984   370'.28'54   83-23070
ISBN 0-8359-0527-6

The final typeset pages composed in Century Schoolbook were produced on a TyXSET 1000 system in Reston, Virginia, using a Mergenthaler Omnitech/2100. The page proofs were produced using a Canon LBP-10 Laser Printer.

TyXSET 1000 is a trademark of TyX Corporation

10 9 8 7 6 5 4 3 2 1

PRINTED IN THE UNITED STATES OF AMERICA

In memory of Sadie Steckler

Contents

Preface

We have all heard that the computer revolution is upon us, the age of information has arrived. We see that computers, already common in many aspects of modern life, are rapidly entering our schools and homes. We hear strong claims and intense debates about the potential effects of these machines upon children's education.

This book is about the possibilities for computers in education, possibilities that are already happening for some students and teachers. Computers can be valuable tools which facilitate current methods of teaching and learning, and they can make entirely new methods feasible. Computers can facilitate teaching and learning for all students, for most topics, and in a wide variety of educational settings. But if used poorly, computers can perpetuate misguided educational practices and create new problems. We need to develop the knowledge and skills necessary to make good use of this powerful new technology.

Brave New Schools: How Computers Can Change Education is intended to help you understand the potential of computers. This book portrays many ways computers can serve education, and it contains detailed descriptions of how students can actually use computers. The examples are placed within a fictional school of the not-so-distant future, which I call Babbage School. (It is named for Charles Babbage, who designed a computer long before the technology to actually build it was available.) While Babbage School is fictional, everything I describe is feasible right now, and the examples reflect experiences of many children and adults who have already used computers in schools, homes, businesses, museums, science centers, libraries and summer camps.

Most of the recent innovations in educational uses of computers involve *personal computers* (also called *microcomputers*). These are the small, relatively inexpensive, self-contained computers that are becoming popular in schools and homes. The personal computers most widely used in education are made by Apple, Atari, Commodore, IBM, Tandy (Radio Shack) and Texas Instruments. Larger computers, called *minicomputers*, and very large computers, called *mainframe computers*, have been used in education since the 1960s and continue to be important for working with large amounts of information. This book focuses primarily upon personal computers, but some uses of larger computers are also covered. In fact, one application of personal computers is to gain access to information stored in larger computers.

This book contains 11 chapters. Chapter 1 presents an overview of Babbage School and diverse examples of how computers can facilitate teaching and learning. Babbage School illustrates how computers can both serve and change education.

Chapter 2 is an introduction to the nature of computers and the main components of computer systems. It covers only the basic concepts and terminology. Readers interested in more information about how computers work should refer to Appendix A.

Chapters 3 through 10 present more detailed descriptions of the educational uses of computers. Each chapter combines general discussion with specific examples of the use of computers at Babbage School.

Chapter 3 focuses on using computers as tools for writing, art and music. Computerized word processing makes creating and revising any type of writing much easier. It encourages students to write, revise and edit more, and thereby leads to improved writing. Students can also use computers as a new means for creating art and music. Computer art makes new possibilities, such as animations and special effects, readily available to children. In music, computers enable students to create their own compositions and experiment with notes and rhythms, even if they have not yet learned to play any instrument.

Chapter 4 discusses computers as tools for gathering, organizing and analyzing information. Personal computers can be connected to large computers via telephone lines and then used to access all sorts of information. This chapter describes, for example, how students can obtain references to all the recent magazine articles about any topic they choose. It also describes how they can use computers to store, organize and analyze information.

Chapter 5 covers computer simulations, which enable students to explore situations and events created within the computer. For example, students can learn about the business world by managing a simulated business. Complex interactions and effects over long periods of time can be simulated almost instantly. Students can perform many types of simulated explorations and experiments that would be too expensive, dangerous, or time consuming to perform in actuality. Simulations encourage active, exploratory learning and they can lead to insights into phenomena that cannot be brought into the classroom in any other way.

Chapter 6 is about playful exercises for the mind. These are games, puzzles and creative tools which help children develop reading, math, memory, problem solving and other mental abilities.

Chapter 7 discusses computerized lessons. Computers make it possible to tailor lessons to be appropriate for each individual. Good instructional programs present information, ask questions, give immediate feedback, provide information to clarify students' misconceptions, and adjust the difficulty and speed of presentation to each student's level.

Chapter 8 focuses on computerized drill and practice. Computers have special advantages for repetitive drill work. They can continuously adjust the level of the drill to be appropriate for each individual, and they can immediately let the student know whether each response was correct or incorrect, slow or fast. Furthermore, computers never show signs of fatigue or impatience, no matter how many repetitions a student needs.

Chapter 9 focuses on computer programming. It discusses the benefits of children learning to program, and describes and compares the two languages, BASIC and Logo, most often used to teach children.

Chapter 10 discusses special uses of computers for blind, deaf, mute and motorically disabled students. It describes how computers can provide disabled people with new means of communicating, learning and working.

Chapter 11 briefly discusses some of the issues and decisions involved in getting started using computers. It also covers the limitations of computers. While computers can be extremely valuable educational tools, they cannot solve all the problems of education.

Appendix A describes the inner workings of computers, for readers interested in more details than are provided in Chapter 2. Appendix B contains notes about the existing computer programs upon which examples in this book are based. It also lists recommended sources of further information. The books, magazines, journals, resource centers, and computerized information systems cited

will enable interested readers to delve further into the topics covered
in this book, as well as keep up with new developments. Following
the appendices, there is a detailed index.

This book is a product of the computer age. It was written with
a word processing program on a Commodore computer. The entire
manuscript was then transferred via a modem and telephone to a
larger computer at TYX Corporation, where camera-ready copy was
produced directly from the computer. All the illustrations except
those in Appendix A were produced with an Apple IIe computer. A
more powerful computer graphics system, the Via Video System I
picture processing system, was used in designing the cover.

While computers provided tools that helped in writing, editing,
illustrating and producing this book, it could have been written
without these machines. But without the encouragement, support
and assistance of many friends and colleagues, it is unlikely I would
have ever started this book and certain that I would never have
been able to finish it.

My work with computers in education began with research projects while I was teaching at the University of Toronto in 1980-
1981. My collaborators in this research, Mary Humphrey and Peter
Lindsay, contributed a great deal to my interest in and thoughts
about the potential of computers for education. Tom Wojdylo and
Fergus Craik also provided invaluable support.

During the summer of 1981, I taught two classes on Personal
Computers in Education at the Ontario Institute for Studies in
Education. The enthusiasm and interest of many of the teachers
attending these classes led me to consider writing a book.

During the two years in which this book came to be, J.B. Shelton
has contributed in innumerable ways. She has patiently tolerated
endless discussions, provided valuable comments and suggestions
on every chapter, proofread the final manuscript, prepared the index and, time and time again, convinced me that I could complete a
worthwhile book. Her enthusiasm, confidence and assistance made
this book possible.

Mary Humphrey has also contributed to this book throughout
the long period of its creation. She read multiple drafts of every
chapter and provided valuable insights about schools, teaching, and
children's learning.

Joanne Koltnow and Jillian Milligan read and critiqued every
chapter. James Bliss, Judy Deken, LeRoy Finkel and William
Steckler each read and critiqued specific chapters. The generosity
of all these people in sharing their expertise and perspectives led
to significant improvements in this book.

The illustrations are a critical part of this book. Those for the *Monster Masher* and *What's Next* programs in Chapter 6 and the biology program in Chapter 7 were created by Jillian Milligan and Connie Chronis. Lucia Grossberger provided the "Gene at the Tunnel" pictures in Chapter 3. Many of the other illustrations are from existing programs. Jillian Milligan helped prepare these.

The book cover was designed by Harry Vertelney and Lucia Grossberger. The cover photographs are by Jillian Milligan.

Carol King of Reston Publishing Company has been an ideal editor: supportive, enthusiastic and patient.

Much of the material in Chapter 1 and some of that in chapters 5 and 8 was published previously in my "Learning with Computers" column in *Compute!* magazine. I thank the editors of *Compute!* for permission to reuse this material.

Finally, I am grateful to the many teachers, parents and children who have shared with me their experiences, views, and aspirations about education and computers.

Palo Alto, California

Chapter 1

A Visit to Babbage School

How might computers change schools in the near future? To answer this question, I describe a visit to a fictional school in which modern technology plays an integral part in teaching and learning. I've named the school in honor of Charles Babbage, who in the 1800s designed a machine similar to modern computers. (Unfortunately, Babbage was never able to build a working version of his "analytic engine.") The guide for our visit is named Ms. Byron, after Babbage's collaborator and financial supporter, Ada Byron. While Babbage School and Ms. Byron are fictional, all the applications of computers I describe are feasible right now. In fact, they are already being used in some schools, homes, research projects and special education centers.

LEARNING AT BABBAGE SCHOOL

The teachers at Babbage School strive to help students develop general research, thinking and communication skills. They emphasize that students should learn to find and use information effectively, rather than try to remember as much as possible. The children at Babbage School work individually and in groups on different lessons and projects. Often they can choose how they will approach learning a topic, as well as when they will work on which lessons. The teachers try to make sure each child engages in a balanced variety of activities each week, while allowing sufficient opportunities for students to emphasize areas of special interest.

1

COMPUTER SIMULATIONS

Students at Babbage School often use computers in their lessons and projects. As a result, many of their learning experiences are very different from those of students in other schools. For example, eleven-year-old Jane showed me a computer lesson on ecology and pollution. The computer displayed a picture of a lake with a variety of plants and fish. It also provided information about the food chain and reproduction rates of the species within the lake. Jane then "told" the computer (by typing answers to the computer's questions) that a certain amount of a pollutant had entered the lake. The computer responded that the pollutant had killed fifty percent of the algae and asked Jane to predict the resulting effects on life in the lake over the next five years.

After making her predictions, Jane compared them to the actual effects calculated by the computer. She found that she had predicted much less damage than would actually occur. She was particularly surprised to find the pollutant resulted in severe damage to the trout, even though it did not harm them directly. When she requested further information, the computer program explained that trout feed upon insects that require algae to survive. By working with this simulation for less than one hour, Jane gained a good understanding of the relationships within the lake ecosystem, and she learned some general principles of ecology.

Another simulation program, called *Oregon Trail*, lets students role-play traveling across the United States in the mid 1800s. Each player is given a limited budget and has to purchase oxen, food, clothing, ammunition and other supplies. Along the way, players decide when to stop at forts, purchase additional supplies, hunt for food or continue on the route. They also have to deal with difficult terrain, bad weather, bandits, and other hazards like those encountered by people in the Gold Rush days. The computer illustrates the progress of the journey, warns about approaching hazards, and asks questions when students have to make decisions. Figure 1.1 shows one of the screen displays. The covered wagon marks the student's current location, and the line marks the route from Missouri to Oregon. The bottom of the display shows the current date and number of miles traveled so far. Ms. Byron said this simulation is much better than a book in getting children to understand the challenges pioneers had to overcome when traveling to the western states.

```
MAY 10 1847              MILES  648

PRESS SPACE BAR TO CONTINUE
```

FIGURE 1.1   Sample display screen from the Oregon Trail
program.

Other science programs available at Babbage School provide
simulations for students to explore aspects of biology, chemistry,
physics, earth science, computer operations and space travel. In
addition, two social studies programs let students simulate directing a presidential campaign and managing a business.

Ms. Byron explained the virtues of simulations:

Children enjoy exploring simulations and they learn a great
deal while doing so. This type of learning makes abstract
concepts more concrete and manageable for children. In
addition, children get more out of learning through active
exploration than they can from just passively remembering
information given to them.

She also noted:

Unfortunately, relatively few good simulation programs are
available, and creating one is a difficult, time-consuming

task. The development of good programs has lagged behind advances in computer equipment ever since I first worked with computers.

EDUCATIONAL COMPUTER GAMES

I was surprised to see children in a classroom playing with a game that looked just like pinball on a computer screen (see Figure 1.2). It turned out to be pinball, but also part of their science lessons. Eleven-year-old Bill explained: "The game program lets you change the world you play in. You can change gravity so it's like playing on the low gravity of an asteroid or make it like playing on the high gravity of a big planet like Jupiter." Bill demonstrated that when he sets gravity low, the ball on the computer screen moves as if it were very light, almost like a ping-pong ball. When he sets gravity high, the ball moves as if it were made of lead. Ms. Byron explained that this program is very successful in helping children understand how gravity and other physical properties

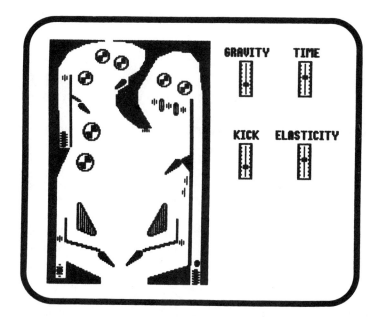

FIGURE 1.2   The computer pinball game. The player can move the markers in the boxes at the right, thereby changing the physics of the world in which the game is played.

affect movement. The children certainly enjoy playing and experimenting with it.

During my visit, I found that students at Babbage School often use educational computer games. Competitive games requiring (and providing practice in) math and language skills are very popular. One example of a math game is called *Maxit*. In this game there is a board with a grid of randomly arranged numbers (see Figure 1.3). Two children play, taking turns selecting numbers by moving a marker on the game board. The first player can only move left or right across the rows of the board to select a number; the second player can only move up or down the columns. When a player selects a number, it is added to his score and removed from the game board. The aim of the game is to accumulate more points than your opponent.

Maxit players plan ahead, trying to take as high a number as they can without leaving their opponent in a position to take a higher one. They also make sure they don't give their opponent an opportunity to leave them in a weak position on a later turn. Playing Maxit therefore requires both strategic thinking and math skills. Twelve-year-old Jennifer explained that you can play against the computer instead of another child. She said the computer was

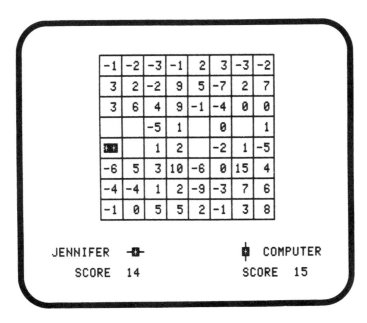

FIGURE 1.3   Maxit game board.

difficult to beat and she was trying to figure out how it was programmed to play so well.

Two children, Jane and Wendy, were playing another game, called *Square Pairs*. This is a version of the memory game called *Concentration*. The computer screen displayed a game board with sixteen boxes (see Figure 1.4). Jane and Wendy took turns trying to find boxes with matching pairs. On each player's turn, she selected two boxes and the computer displayed the contents of each. When a player found a match, a point was added to her score and she received another turn.

To win at Square Pairs, players have to remember what is in each box as it is uncovered and recognize when pairs match. In the game Jane and Wendy were playing, the pairs were French phrases and their English translations. Wendy said they had just finished playing with another set of matches, countries and capital cities. Jane explained that the best part of the program is that you can make your own games with any types of matches you want and you can decide how many matches to have in your game.

Several children were playing an *adventure game* in which they explored a fantasy world created within the computer, searching

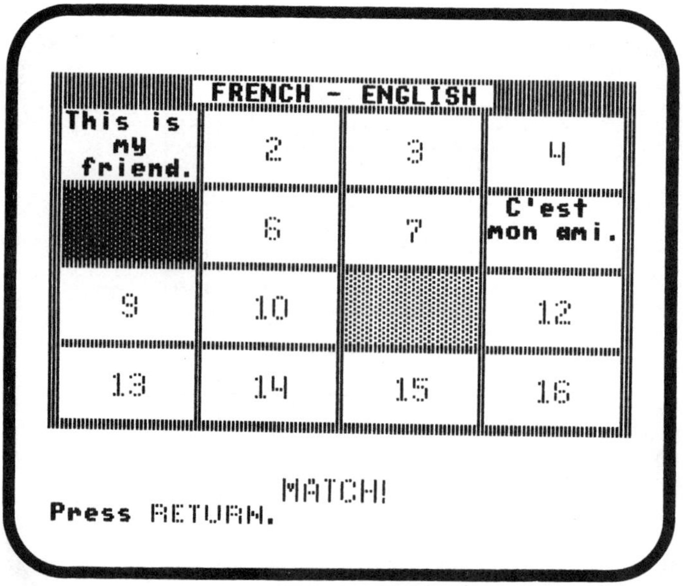

FIGURE 1.4   Square Pairs game board. A match has just been found.

for treasure in castles, caves and mazes, while trying to avoid the dangers of creatures such as wizards, dragons and gremlins. Lessons in reading comprehension, logical problem solving, and map usage were embedded within the game. Ms. Byron told me some children spend a lot of time with these game/lessons. Sometimes they spend many sessions over several weeks to complete one adventure.

Some of the adventure game programs have been designed to let teachers add to them. These games contain a wizard who can appear at any time and ask the players a question. If the players give the correct answer, they will be rewarded with a hint that will help them find a treasure. But if they give an incorrect answer, they might lose a treasure they have found or have an evil spell cast upon them. The teachers can enter questions for the wizard to ask, along with the answers that will be accepted as correct. They use this capability to introduce educational material and to motivate students to do other lessons. For example, twelve-year-old James (who told me that "Adventure is a real classic computer game") often neglected his science lessons. One teacher had the wizard in James' favorite adventure game ask him questions about star constellations. James knew he needed to answer the questions to find all the treasures in the game. Later, I saw him engrossed in an astronomy lesson.

COMPUTERIZED READING LESSONS

I also observed a surprising use of computers for children's reading lessons. Seven-year-old Robbie was reading a story displayed on the computer screen. Once in a while, he would use a joystick (like those used with video games) to move a marker on the computer screen. Robbie moved the marker to a word, pressed the joystick button, and the computer pronounced the word aloud. Its pronunciations were not always perfect, but they were clear enough for Robbie to understand. Ms. Byron explained that the computer is programmed to provide help when the child does not know a word. This is especially beneficial for children who have reading difficulties, since it avoids the problem of their getting stuck on a few words and therefore not trying to understand the story. Ms. Byron also said this program motivates children to read and helps them learn new words. The computer keeps a record of the words each child tells it to pronounce. The teachers use these records to help them decide when children are ready for more advanced reading materials.

WRITING WITH COMPUTERS

Several students were engaged in writing projects. All their writing was done using computers with a word processing program. The word processing program made it easy for them to enter and revise their writing. While working on the computers, students correct spelling errors; add, delete and rearrange words, sentences and paragraphs; and make other revisions. When they finish their writing, they have the computer print what they have written. The computer automatically sets proper margins, numbers pages, and underlines and centers designated words.

Ms. Byron said that a good word processing program makes writing more enjoyable, so the children write more often and produce longer essays. They are also willing to revise their work many times — something they are reluctant to do when they have to rewrite by hand. One child told me he likes to write on the computer "because it always looks neat and is easy to change. It doesn't hurt your hand and you can print out copies of what you write to give to everybody."

Ms. Byron pointed out that word processing programs let children try different combinations of words and arrangements of sentences, and then select the ones they like best. She is planning to add other programs to assist in writing. One will provide an "online" dictionary and thesaurus so students can check their spellings and find synonyms with the computer. Another special program is designed for writing poetry. It includes a dictionary of rhymes and a selection of formats in which poems can be printed.

I was surprised that all the children knew how to type so well. Ms. Byron explained that they had learned typing with a computer program. The computer presents typing drills, students do the drills on the keyboard, and the computer keeps detailed records of their speed and accuracy. The computer then gives each student additional practice on those letters and letter combinations he had typed slowly or incorrectly. Since practice for each individual focuses on the specific letters and sequences he found difficult, the student rapidly acquires typing skills.

Some of the children were writing articles and stories for the school newspaper. Antonio told me he was writing a science fiction story about what the world would be like without any computers. When he finished the story, he stored a copy on the school's central computer for the editor of the newspaper to read. The editor was not at school the day Antonio finished his story, but had promised to connect to the school's computer from her home computer to check Antonio's story. She would then leave her comments stored in the computer so Antonio could read them and revise the story whenever he had time. When all the students finish their articles and stories, the editor uses the computer to format and print the newspaper.

Other children were using computerized word processing to write letters. They told me the letters were for their pen-pals in Mexico. They use a computer, a telephone and a special device called a *modem* to send the letters to a large central computer. The students in Mexico use a similar system to receive the letters. This is called *electronic mail,* and the students pointed out that no paper is used. The letters would arrive quickly and the children expected to receive answers the next day. One student asked why the children they wrote to were called "pen-pals" when no pen was used to communicate with them. After I explained, another child added: "It's like why we say 'dial the phone' when we really push buttons — it's left over from the old days."

COMPUTER INFORMATION BASES

Some children were preparing for a debate as part of their current events lessons. They used a computer, telephone and modem to connect to the computer in their local library. They could then use a computerized index of the books and periodicals available. Pam explained that you enter a name and the computer tells you which books and articles have information about that person, place, or thing. Jill added that you could do "trickier things." For example, she only wanted articles that discussed both solar energy and nuclear energy, and had been published within the last two years. She easily instructed the computer to list the appropriate references. She also pointed out they could use many different *information bases,* including the *New York Times Index,* the *Guide to Periodical Literature* and the *United Press International Reports,* all from the computers in their own classroom. Their teacher said that knowing how to use computers to get information is as important as knowing how to use an encyclopedia or a library.

COMPUTERIZED DRILL AND PRACTICE

The children at Babbage School spend some time on more traditional lessons and drills, but many of these also involve computers. I observed one computerized lesson that taught children about map reading. The computer displayed a map and questions for the student to answer (see Figure 1.5). The student answered some questions by typing on the keyboard and others by pointing at the map on the computer screen with a device called a *light pen*. The computer program could tell whether the light pen was pointed at the appropriate location on the map. When the child answered questions incorrectly, the computer provided hints and explanations. When the child answered a set of questions correctly, the computer displayed a more complex map and asked more difficult questions.

In another class, a child named Seymour was using a spelling drill program. An audio tape recorder was connected to the computer. After Seymour got the tape recorder ready, he pressed the RETURN key on the computer keyboard. The computer started the tape recorder, which played a message previously recorded by the teacher: "The first word is *receive*. I like to receive presents. Receive." Seymour typed the word, but misspelled it as *recieve*. The computer immediately responded with *rec — — ve*, showing that he had made a mistake on the two blank letters. Seymour typed the missing letters and studied the correct spelling. When he pressed

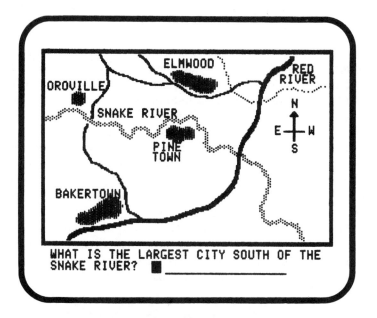

FIGURE 1.5 Sample display screen from the map tutorial program.

the RETURN key, the computer erased the word and displayed a message asking him to spell it again. He spelled it correctly and proceeded to the next word. At the end of the drill, the computer printed lists of the words Seymour had spelled correctly and those he had misspelled. One of the teachers said children learn quickly with this spelling program, since they have to correct their errors immediately and retype the entire word before going on.

COMPUTERS AS VISUAL AIDS

Teachers also use computers as visual aids while they explain material. For example, in an eighth grade math lesson, Ms. Marcus was explaining how formulas can be graphed. She had a computer with a large display screen that everyone could see. As she typed each formula, the computer automatically displayed the appropriate graph. The program let her display several formulas at the same time, so students could see how they compare. Figure 1.6 shows an example of the display after she had entered two formulas, $Y = 2 * SIN(X)$ and $Y = SIN(2 * X)$. Ms. Marcus finds using this program to be much more convenient and accurate than drawing the graphs on transparencies or a chalk board. In addition, when students ask how a certain formula would be graphed Ms. Marcus simply types it into the computer and the correct graph quickly appears on the screen.

COMPUTER AIDS FOR HANDICAPPED CHILDREN

I noticed a child wearing headphones that were connected to a small box next to a computer. The box was a *speech synthesizer*. At the push of a button, it produced a spoken version of the written text on the screen. Ms. Byron explained that John has been blind since birth, but with the speech synthesizer and other electronic devices he is able to progress with his lessons very well. She emphasized that computers have been a tremendous help in educating children with all types of handicaps and in making it possible for handicapped children to work in regular classes.

Several children who receive part of their education at Babbage School have severe physical handicaps. They are able to work with computers by using special devices. Ms. Byron showed me a computer program that displays the alphabet on the computer

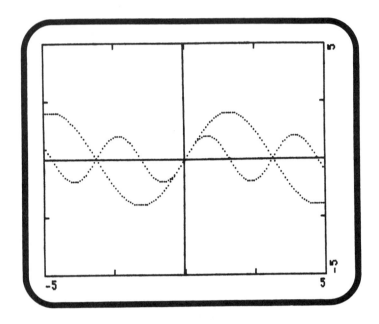

FIGURE 1.6   Computer-generated graphs. The teacher had entered
two equations, Y = 2 * SIN(X) and Y = SIN(2 * X).

screen. A marker moves along the letters at an adjustable speed. The student presses a switch to select the letter the marker is on, and this letter is then placed in a special display area of the screen. In this way, the student can create a written message. The student can have the computer print a copy of the message, send it to another computer via electronic mail, or pronounce the words with a speech synthesizer.

A severely disabled child named Bill could not speak or control his arm movements well enough to write or type. However, he was able to use this system with a specially designed switch. When Bill was first learning to use this system, the marker was programmed to move very slowly over the letters. As he became more proficient, his teacher made a simple change in the program so the marker moved more quickly. Bill now uses this computer system to do his assignments as well as to create messages for the teachers and other children. He is particularly excited about being able to communicate with other people using a computerized message system. He wrote a message that said, "It's almost like using a phone."

CREATIVE USES OF COMPUTERS

Computer studies are a standard part of the curriculum at Babbage School and many lessons are about computers. In addition, all the children learn to use computers to do original creative work. Some children create their own programs; others use computers in creating pictures or music.

One group of three children were creating a math drill program to be used by younger children in the school. After having some six-year-olds test it, they told me that it was "a neat program, but some of the instructions mixed up the little kids. We have to make it more user-friendly."

Two other children were writing programs to create interesting designs on the computer screen. They said they used a computer language called Logo. To show me one of their designs, they typed into the computer:

MANYSQUARES 8

The pattern shown in Figure 1.7A appeared on the computer screen. The children explained that the same program can make many different patterns. All you have to do is type MANYSQUARES followed by a number. Some of their other designs are shown in Figures 1.7B, 1.7C and 1.7D.

I asked to see the program, and the children instructed the computer to list it on the screen. The entire program consisted of:

```
TO SQUARE
    REPEAT 4 [FORWARD 50 RIGHT 90]
END


TO MANYSQUARES :NUMBER
    REPEAT :NUMBER [SQUARE RIGHT 360/:NUMBER]
END
```

I expressed my surprise that the program was so short. The students said they had started with a more complex, longer program and had worked to make it better. They were proud of how efficient it was now.

Other children were composing music on a computer. They used a program that let them enter numeric codes for notes, listen to the music, alter its pitch and tempo, and change the notes. This program is in many ways similar to the word processing program, but it is for creating and editing music rather than essays. When

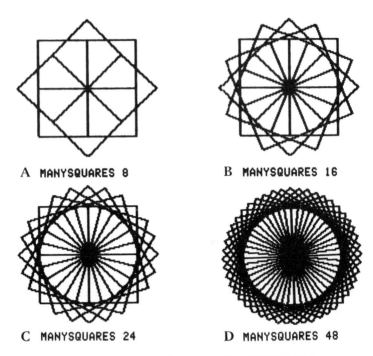

A MANYSQUARES 8 B MANYSQUARES 16

C MANYSQUARES 24 D MANYSQUARES 48

FIGURE 1.7   Patterns created with the MANYSQUARES program.

they finished creating their song, the children sent it (via electronic mail) to be entered in a statewide computer music contest. The judges of the contest would use their own computer to listen to all the songs submitted.

I also observed a group of three children working on a computer art project. Each child took a turn adding to the picture displayed on the screen. They drew on a special board connected to the computer. They simply outlined what they wanted to draw, and it appeared on the screen. After placing a shape on the screen, they gave the computer commands to color, move, rotate, erase and change the size of the shape. With a great deal of debate (one of the teachers had to ask them to settle down) they gradually created a picture. Later, they had the computer print a large version to hang on the classroom wall and three small copies to take home. One of the children expressed disappointment that they could only print black-and-white copies, since the school did not yet have a color printer. A teacher promised to bring his camera to school and take color photographs of the computer screens with their art work.

VIDEO DISKS AND COMPUTERS

Twelve-year-old Bob was also interested in art and was fascinated by art history. He was using a device recently acquired by

14

the school, a video disk player. A video disk is about the size of a record album, but it can store an enormous number of pictures and sounds. Bob told me one disk can hold over 50,000 individual pictures or an entire full length movie. The video disk player displays the pictures in full color on a television screen. Pictures can be displayed in any order and at any speed. For example, while watching a movie shown on a video disk player, you can play sections in fast or slow motion, repeat or skip parts, and even run the movie backwards.

The video disk player at Babbage School was connected to a computer. Bob was using a special art history package that included both a video disk and a computer program. The program contained an index to the pictures on the video disk, so the computer could be used to control which pictures were shown. Bob displayed pictures by typing the artist's name or the title of a particular painting. He said you could also select pictures in other ways, such as by the country or time period in which they were painted. Bob gave me a quick demonstration of the similarities between some of Picasso's drawings and primitive cave art. He was able to bring the relevant pictures to the screen within a matter of seconds. He was thrilled by having an entire history of art at his fingertips.

TEACHERS' VIEWS OF COMPUTER LEARNING

The teachers at Babbage School spend most of their time with individuals or small groups of children. Computers have made lessons, grading and record keeping more efficient, so teachers have more time to assist students with particular problems, create new lessons, guide and encourage students, and learn new things themselves. They realize that computers can never replace them, but can serve valuable educational functions. Ms. Byron told me, "Computerized lessons are somewhere between learning from a teacher and learning from a book. The computer is more interactive and adaptive to the students than a book, but much less so than a good teacher."

The teachers use computers to help make instruction fit the level, pace and learning style of each student. Their emphasis on individualized instruction has led to a de-emphasis of grading and comparing students. This, in turn, has encouraged students to engage in more cooperative learning, peer tutoring and collaborative projects. Students at Babbage School interact with each other and their teachers more than in most schools.

Mr. Brown, who had been teaching for twenty years, told me that many problems are minimized when education becomes more individualized and active. Students and teachers feel less frustration and a greater sense of accomplishment when there is so much flexibility in the content and methods of teaching and learning. The students enjoy the emphasis on active, exploratory learning. Children with learning problems receive a great deal of help, since teachers have time for individual tutoring while computers provide unlimited practice at a level and pace appropriate for each child. Different teaching methods can be used for each student, and the teachers aim to find a method to suit each individual. As a result, the problems that could lead to a child being labeled as "learning disabled" have been greatly reduced.

The teachers were careful to point out that while computers are extremely valuable educational tools, they do not solve all the problems of education. For example, computers cannot decide which lessons should be part of the school curriculum, nor can they insure that each student participates in a good balance of activities. The teachers also said that using computers has not always been easy. They had to learn a great deal, and they have all experienced disappointing programs, faulty equipment, misleading claims made by computer companies, and other difficulties. However, every teacher and student at Babbage School is now proficient at using computers. Some of the teachers even create their own lesson programs for students to use.

Incorporating computers into education at Babbage School has been a gradual process. Several years ago, a few teachers began using computers for drills and lessons. After becoming comfortable with computers and knowledgeable about the possibilities, they introduced simulations and word processing. Simulations and word processing showed the other teachers that computers opened new possibilities for education. This led many of them who were skeptical at first to become interested in trying computers in their own classes. Gradually, computers were incorporated into more types of lessons, and completely new learning experiences were introduced. Everyone has been especially excited by the success of the special education teachers in using computers with handicapped children.

Integrating computers into teaching and learning at Babbage School required many people to spend a lot of time and effort, but all the teachers and students believe it has been well worth it. They continue to explore new ways in which technology can serve education.

Chapter 2

The Nature
of Computers

Computers influence our lives every day. They play a role in our work, education, recreation and communications. Bank tellers, travel agents, secretaries, bookkeepers, journalists, insurance agents, stock brokers, sales clerks, telephone operators, teachers, students and others use computers every day. Yet for many people these machines are shrouded in mystery.

There are two main points that are essential to begin understanding computers. The first is that computers are tools for working with information — words, numbers, pictures and sounds. Tools expand our capabilities. Some tools, such as hammers and pulleys, expand our *physical* capabilities. Other tools, such as telescopes and telephones, expand our *sensory* capabilities. Computers are tools that expand our *mental* capabilities.

Other machines, such as tape recorders and calculators, also help us with information. However, each of these machines is limited to performing specific operations (such as storage or calculation) upon specific types of information (such as sounds or numbers). The advantage of computers is that they can perform a wide variety of processes upon all types of information. Computers can help us store, retrieve, organize, compare, modify, communicate, and analyze words, numbers, pictures and sounds.

The second important point about computers is that in order to do anything at all, they must be given instructions in the form of a *program*. A program is a set of detailed, step-by-step instructions, written in a language the computer can process. Computers obey the instructions in a program exactly. They have no common sense or knowledge of how things are typically done. They cannot interpret vague or ambiguous instructions, no matter how obvious it would be to a person. Therefore, whenever you read or hear "The computer did..." you should interpret it to mean "The computer was programmed to do..."

Each program tells the computer how to perform certain functions. The remarkable flexibility of computers is due to the fact that they can follow the instructions of different programs. We can create an infinite variety of programs for any computer and choose when to use each one.

COMPUTERS AS EDUCATIONAL TOOLS

The flexible information processing capability of computers makes them potentially useful in a wide variety of educational applications. They can facilitate teaching and learning at all levels, from preschool children mastering the alphabet to doctors learning new diagnostic techniques. They can be used in all subjects — language as well as math, history as well as science, vocational training as well as business education, music and art as well as reading and writing. Computers open new ways of developing thinking and problem solving skills, and they provide new possibilities for learning through active exploration. They can make lessons, drills, tests and record keeping more efficient, thereby, freeing teachers to spend more time providing individualized instruction. They can make many types of lessons more interesting and motivating for students, and they can make enormous amounts of information readily available. Computers can be programmed to display pictures and animations, play music, perform calculations, serve as sophisticated typewriters, analyze class records, translate written words to speech, measure response times, control tape recorders and video disk players, and provide a medium for creativity and playful learning.

The possibilities for using computers in education are boundless. Their widespread availability could lead to fundamental changes in classroom teaching and learning, more successful remediation of learning problems, new means of educating handicapped individuals, and expanded opportunities for self-directed and home-based education.

In addition to their potential as learning and teaching aids, computers themselves have become important objects of study. An understanding of their capabilities and limitations is essential for every informed person.

Computers are tools. They are different from other tools in that they operate upon information and can be programmed to serve a wide variety of purposes. But they are the same as other tools in that they can be used well or poorly. A hammer can be used in building furniture or in destroying it. A computer can be used in creating original stories, music and art; in exploring complex scientific relationships; or in playing the most mindless of games. How computers affect students depends upon how the students use them.

ADVANTAGES OF COMPUTERS AS EDUCATIONAL TOOLS

Computers are not the first technological innovation to gain widespread attention in education. Teaching machines, television and films have been promoted as major educational advances. These prior innovations have not fulfilled their advocates' expectations, and it is worthwhile to ask why computers should be expected to have more success.

One advantage of computers is their flexibility. The teaching machines of the 1960s imposed one way of learning — step-by-step structured learning in which students had to answer each question correctly before they could go on to the next one. Computers can be used for this type of instruction, but they can also be used to encourage active, exploratory learning; to individualize material to suit each student; for writing, music and art; and in many other ways. Computers have the potential to do more than make current teaching methods more effective: They open entirely new possibilities for teaching and learning.

Another advantage of computers is they can be programmed to respond to students' actions. Unlike books, television programs or films, computers can provide immediate feedback to students' answers, repeat or elaborate information for students who are doing poorly, jump ahead to more difficult material for students who are doing well, and allow each student to work at his or her own pace. Computers can always be ready to respond to answers from the quickest students, yet always repeat things and wait for answers from the slowest students. If used well, computers can make truly individualized learning possible — each student learning in his own way, at a comfortable pace, working with material that is well suited to his abilities and prior knowledge.

Current claims about computers can be compared to prior claims about the educational potential of television, and this comparison raises serious concerns. Computers in education are now at a stage similar to that of television several decades ago. The enormous educational potential of television is well established; most children have learned a great deal from television. Unfortunately, much of what they have learned consists of advertising jingles and other trivia. With a few notable exceptions, television has not fulfilled its potential as an educational tool. The same could happen with computers; they could end up being used primarily as mindless electronic toys. Since computers are just beginning to be widely used, the directions we set in the next few years will be critical in determining whether their potential as educational tools will ever be fulfilled.

HARDWARE COMPONENTS OF A COMPUTER SYSTEM

The knowledge necessary to successfully use computers is no more extensive or complex than that necessary to drive a car. As all cars have steering wheels, brakes, lights, and other standard parts, every computer system has certain components. This section presents brief descriptions of the main components found in all computer systems.

Input and Output

You have probably observed bank tellers, airline ticket agents, and other workers using computers. The visible parts of their computer systems are a typewriter-like keyboard and either a printer or a display screen similar to a television set. The teller or ticket agent communicates with the computer by typing information, such as your account number or travel destination. The typewriter keyboard is the *input component* of the computer system. The computer responds by providing information such as the balance in your account or the schedule of flights to your destination. This information is either printed on paper or displayed on the screen. The printer or screen is the *output component* of the computer system.

Many different devices can serve as input and output components. Typewriter keyboards, used for entering letters and numbers, are the most common input devices. Joysticks, such as those used with video games, are another type of frequently used input device. Joysticks input the position in which the stick is held (e.g., forward, back, left, or right) and whether or not a button is pressed. Other input devices include bar code scanners (used in many supermarkets), light pens (for pointing to selections displayed on the computer screen) and devices for accepting spoken input. Output devices include printers, display screens, speech synthesizers (which enable computers to produce spoken output) and plotters (which enable computers to print color pictures).

Memory

Consider what happens when the ticket agent types your destination and the computer responds with a schedule of flights, or when the bank teller types your account number and the computer responds with your balance. In each case, the computer provides some information that must have been stored within it. Computers have *memory components* for storing information.

There are three types of memory components in a computer system, each serving a different purpose. One is for information permanently stored within the computer, one is for information temporarily stored within the computer, and one is for information stored external to the computer.

Some information, such as the rules for adding and subtracting numbers, is used so often we want to have it permanently stored in the computer and immediately available at all times. Permanent information is stored in *read only memory* or ROM. Information in ROM is built into the computer so it is available as soon as the computer is turned on. This information can be retrieved ("read") and used, but it cannot be changed except by changing a physical part of the computer. You can think of information in ROM as etched in stone: In order to change it, the stone must be replaced.

Some computer systems use ROMs on plug-in cartridges, so they can be replaced conveniently. The information within the ROM cartridge cannot be changed; the entire cartridge has to be removed and replaced.

Other information needs to be stored temporarily and changed often. For example, each time you deposit or withdraw money, the record of your account in the bank's computer must be altered. Another example is computer programs that are placed in the computer's temporary internal memory as they are needed. This allows us to alter programs and easily replace one program with another. Temporary, changeable information is stored in *random access memory* or RAM. You can think of information in RAM as written with chalk: It can be changed easily and is not saved permanently. In fact, for most computers all information in RAM is lost whenever the computer is turned off.

When we type a program or information into a computer, it is stored in RAM. However, we generally do not want to lose the information when the computer is turned off. Also, in many cases we will have more information than can fit in the computer's RAM at one time. We therefore need the third type of memory: *external memory*. You can think of external memory as the computer's filing cabinet. We can have the computer transfer information from RAM into external memory, store it indefinitely, and quickly put it back into RAM when needed.

There are three types of external memory devices commonly used with personal computers: *cassette tape recorders*, *floppy disk drives*, and *hard disk drives*. No matter which is used, we can have an unlimited number of storage elements (i.e., tapes or disks), so any amount of information can be stored. The information remains stored on the tape or disk until it is erased.

Cassette tape recorders are the least expensive type of external memory device available, but they have certain disadvantages. Each tape is limited in how much information it can hold. In addition, information transfer between a cassette tape and the computer is too slow for many purposes.

Floppy disk drives are more expensive than cassette tape recorders, but they have important advantages. Each floppy disk can hold far more information than a cassette tape, floppy disks tend to be more reliable than tape (i.e., information is less likely to be lost), and information is transferred far more quickly than with cassette tapes.

Hard disk drives are even faster and more reliable than floppy disk drives, and they have a much greater storage capacity. They are also much more expensive. Because hard disk drives have such a large capacity and high speed of information transfer, a single one can often serve as the external memory for several personal computers.

Central Processing Unit

Computers do more than simply store and retrieve information; they also process it. For example, after the bank teller enters your account number and the amount of a deposit, the computer calculates your new balance, automatically adding the appropriate interest. That is, the computer performs processes that change the information. The component responsible for processing is called the *central processing unit* or *CPU*. The CPU is the component that follows the programs' instructions.

Personal computers were made possible by the development of the technology to put central processing units (CPU) and internal memories (ROM and RAM) on small, inexpensive pieces of silicon. These remarkable *chips* are the electronic workers of the computer age.

Buses and Interfaces

Input, output, memory and processing are necessary components of every computer system. To work together—to be a system—these components must interact or communicate. For example, when your bank account number is entered, the CPU retrieves your balance from memory, adds or subtracts appropriate amounts, and sends the result back to memory and to the output component.

The components of the computer system are physically linked together by *buses* and *interfaces*. Buses connect the internal components of the computer— RAM, ROM, and CPU. Interfaces connect the internal components with input, output and external memory devices. Special interfaces have also been built to let output signals from a computer turn lights on and off, control video tape recorders and video disks, and work other types of electronic devices.

Input devices, output devices, ROM, RAM, external memory, a CPU, buses, and interfaces are the main *hardware* or physical components of a computer system. While these components are essential for every complete computer system, something more is needed for the computer to be useful.

COMPUTER SOFTWARE

In order to serve any function, a computer must have a suitable program. Programs, which consist of instructions to the computer, are called *software* to contrast them with the hardware components just described. A computer without software is as useless as a camera without film or a lamp without a light bulb.

A program must be placed in the internal memory of a computer in order for the CPU to follow the instructions. Programs can be permanently placed within ROM memory when the computer is built, stored on a ROM cartridge and plugged into the computer when needed (on some systems), or temporarily placed within RAM memory. Whether a program is put into ROM or RAM is determined by how often it will be needed and whether it is likely to need revisions.

Software is often divided into two categories: *applications software* and *system software*. Applications programs are those which have the computer serve different functions—word processing, drill and practice, lessons, games, simulations, and so on. That is, each program provides instructions that enable the computer to be used for a specific task. Applications programs are almost always stored on tape, disk or ROM cartridge, and loaded into the computer when needed. Any number of different applications programs can be used with a computer, but only one can be used at a time.

Systems software controls general operations within the computer, operations that are essential for many different applications. For example, an *operating system* coordinates all the activities of the hardware components, making sure the proper information is sent to each component at the appropriate time. Another type of system software is *computer language translators* (more technically called *interpreters* and *compilers*). These are programs that translate programming languages that are relatively easy for people to use into the *machine language* required by the CPU (see Appendix A for further discussion). Systems software is often built into ROM in the computer, although it can also be loaded into RAM.

HOW COMPUTERS WORK

You do not have to know about the internal workings of computers in order to use them successfully, any more than you have to know about the internal workings of automobiles in order to drive. For interested readers, Appendix A contains a discussion of how information is represented and processed within a computer. This section simply summarizes the key points.

At their most fundamental level of operation, computers distinguish between only two different symbols, which are referred to as 0 and 1. This is a convenient and reliable system: Inside the computer, the 0s and 1s are coded as two electrical states. All information in the computer, whether numbers, words, pictures or sounds, is represented by sequences of these two symbols. This two-symbol system is called the *binary* system. Each 0 or 1 is called *bit*, which is a shortened form of *binary digit*. Many computers operate on groups of eight bits at a time, so a group of eight bits is given a special name: a *byte*.

Within the computer, all processes are built from a few very simple operations that are performed by electronic devices called *logic gates*. Logic gates perform their operations upon bits. For example, one type of logic gate changes 0s to 1s and 1s to 0s. The simple, fundamental operations of the logic gates are combined and recombined to build all the complex operations computers perform. An example of how more complex computer operations are built from simpler ones is given in Appendix A.

LIMITATIONS OF COMPUTERS

While computers are powerful and flexible tools, they do have limitations. The most important limitation is that any computer, even the largest and most powerful one, is limited to those functions someone can program it to perform. Every year, more sophisticated programs are developed, extending the capabilities of computers. However, we are still a long way from knowing how to create many desirable programs. For example, no one has been able to program a computer to understand English (or any other natural language) even as well as a young child. Similarly, no one has been able to program a computer to translate between any two languages nearly as well as a person who knows both languages. We do not know enough about how people understand language to instruct a computer in all the details of how it is to be done. Likewise, we are not able to program computers to emulate human creativity, insight, intuition or emotions.

Personal computers have many more limitations than large, mainframe computers. Personal computers are more limited in the amount of information they can handle at one time and how quickly they can process it. These limitations are clearly seen in such areas as the quality of pictures that can be produced on the screen, the speed and sophistication of animations, and the capabilities to produce and understand speech. As you read in the following chapters about the varied uses of personal computers, it is important to remember that there are many limitations to their capabilities and they can only do what they are programmed to do.

Chapter 3

Creating with Computers: Writing, Art and Music

Computers with appropriate software are powerful tools for creative expression in writing, art and music. Word processing programs remove much of the tedium of writing and editing, thereby encouraging more and better writing. Graphics creation programs facilitate the creation of pictures, animations and special visual effects. Music composition programs open new possibilities for exploring music, even for people who do not know how to play an instrument.

Many word processing, graphics creation and music composition programs are available for personal computers. In this chapter, I describe how these types of programs can serve valuable educational functions. I use examples placed within the fictional context of Babbage School, but they are all based upon existing programs. Appendix B lists the titles and sources of these programs.

WRITING WITH COMPUTERS

Writing requires two types of activities: the mental processes of composing sentences to convey the intended meanings and the physical processes of putting words onto paper. Computerized word processing makes the physical processes easier, so they do not distract the writer from the mental processes. A word processor enables the writer to devote more effort and attention to the text he is composing, and less to actions such as typing, erasing, cutting and pasting.

When using a word processing program, you type on the computer keyboard and the words appear on the display screen. You can quickly and easily correct typing mistakes; insert, delete and rearrange letters, words and sentences; find and replace particular words or phrases; and make other changes. At any time, you can have the computer print a clean, well-formatted copy of your work. The computer will follow your instructions for setting margins and line spacing, centering headings, underlining key words, printing page numbers, and so on.

Word processing programs can be combined with *spelling check programs* that automatically check whether each word in the text matches a word in a computerized dictionary. They can also be integrated with information and communication systems so, for example, messages prepared on a word processor can be sent directly to other computers without ever being printed on paper.

Word processing is the most popular application of computers in business, and it is rapidly gaining popularity in schools and homes. Many word processing programs are available for personal computers. They vary in the number of options and commands available and in how easy they are to use. The more sophisticated programs make personal computers function much like the word processing machines used in many offices. (In fact, word processing machines are actually computers that have word processing programs permanently stored within them.) Simpler word processing programs have been developed for children and for adults who use them only occasionally.

The teachers, secretaries and administrators at Babbage School use computers for most of their writing. Word processing saves them time and effort in office work and in producing materials for students. The students also use word processing, and they enjoy writing with the computer. The ease of entering, revising and printing essays encourages students to write more, edit more, produce better essays, and take greater pride in their work.

One Student's Use of Word Processing

John, a thirteen-year-old student at Babbage School, is one of many who benefit from computerized word processing. John's penmanship is poor and he must struggle to write legibly. Before he began using computerized word processing, he hated to write. When assigned to write an essay, he would try to think out the whole thing in his head, so he would only have to write it once. He often noticed things he would like to change but did not change them, since he would then have to copy the whole essay over. His reluctance to edit his work resulted in poor essays. John also has trouble spelling, and when he writes by hand he frequently has to stop and check a dictionary. This causes him to lose the flow of his thinking and writing. John has often been upset because teachers criticized his papers for being sloppy and containing misspellings. He felt the teachers did not care about what he wrote, but only about whether it looked neat. Using a typewriter helped John some, but he still had to erase typing mistakes, stop to check words in a dictionary, and retype a whole page when he wanted to change just one or two sentences.

During the last year, John has become proficient at using a simple word processing program called the *Bank Street Writer*™. He enjoys writing with it, and both the quantity and quality of his writing have improved significantly.

The Bank Street Writer program has three modes: *write mode*, *edit mode*, and *transfer mode*. Write mode is used to type the words into the computer. Edit mode is used to make changes, such as rearranging paragraphs or erasing unwanted words and sentences. Transfer mode is used to save the writing on a disk and to obtain printed copies. John can easily instruct the computer to switch from one mode to another.

When the program starts in write mode, the computer shows several prompts at the top of the screen (see Figure 3.1). These tell John that the computer is ready for him to enter text, and remind him which keys to use to erase and to go to the edit mode menu (to choose an editing command). Below these prompts, there is a box in which John can enter his essay. Within the box, there is an underline marker called the *cursor* (from the Latin for "runner"). Each time John types a character, it appears at the cursor and the cursor moves to the next position. When he gets to the end of a line, the cursor moves to the beginning of the next line. If John begins a word that does not completely fit on a line, the computer automatically moves the whole word to the next line.

When the cursor gets to the bottom of the box, the display *scrolls* up to make room for more text. That is, the top line of the display moves off the screen, all the other lines move up, and a

FIGURE 3.1   The word processing program in write mode. No text has been entered yet.

new line appears at the bottom. This movement is very quick, so it does not interfere with typing.

John can also control the position of the cursor with special *cursor control keys*. When he moves the cursor to the top line, the screen display scrolls down. John uses the cursor control keys to go back and see what he has typed. He explained that the computer screen is like a window that you can move up and down to see what you have written.

John does not have to worry about margins, line spacing or pages when he enters the text, as he can tell the computer how to set them when he has it print his essay. The computer will then arrange the words into lines of the right length and pages of the right size. If John decides to print another copy with a different format, he can instruct the computer to do so with a few simple commands.

John used many of the word processing program's capabilities to write an essay he called "The World Without Computers." The first thing he wanted to do was type the title, his name and the date, and have these centered on the page. To tell the computer to center a line of text, John held down a special CONTROL key and typed the letter *C*. The computer then displayed the word CENTER in a highlighted block at the beginning of the line (see Figure 3.2). John typed the title of his essay and pressed the RETURN key, which tells the computer to go to a new line. Likewise, he used the centering command on the next line and typed his name, and then did the same thing for the date. The lines were not centered on the screen, but the computer will center them when the essay is printed, automatically adjusting for whatever width margins John sets.

John noticed a typing mistake in the word *world*, which he had typed as *wrold*. He used the cursor control keys to move the cursor to the *r*, and then used the ERASE key to delete the *r* and *o*. He retyped them in the correct order. Erasing and rewriting are much quicker with a word processor than with a pen, pencil or typewriter.

FIGURE 3.2 The word processing program after the first two lines have been entered. The computer will center the lines when it prints the essay.

Also, no matter how much is erased and changed, the final essay will be perfectly formatted and neatly printed.

John then moved the cursor back to where he wanted to begin the story and typed his first two paragraphs:

> Can you imagine what the world would be like without computers? I don't see how anything would ever get done. Suppose when we went to the bank they had to do everything without computers. How would they ever get everything done without computers? How would the airlines ever keep track of all the flights? How could they ever do a survey or a senses? How would the stock market people ever keep track of all the money? How would the telephone company ever funcshion? How many operators would they need to get all the calls conected?
>
> I use computers almost every day. I like to write with a computer because it is real eazy to make changes and the printout always looks real neat. I like to create pictures on the computer too. It is espesially fun because my folks gave me a program for Christmas. I had tried to write my own program and it was OK, but I couldn't get things to move real fast. I like to make cartoons for my little brother and sister to watch. Computers are interesting and a lot of fun. When I did not have a computer I used to spend a lot of time watching TV.

While typing, John caught several small errors and immediately corrected them, so they are not shown above. After typing these paragraphs, he paused to reread them. He wasn't sure how to spell some words, but planned to check them when he was finished writing. He noticed that the second and fourth sentences of his first paragraph said almost exactly the same thing, and he decided to delete the fourth one. He pressed the key marked ESC (for "escape") to tell the computer he wanted to use *edit mode*. The computer then changed the information at the top of the screen to display the editing options (see Figure 3.3). The options showed John that he could *erase, move, find* or *replace* text. If he erased or moved something and then changed his mind, he could use the *unerase* and *moveback* options to change the essay back. The final option shown was to go to the *transfer menu* to use the disk or printer.

One choice on the menu was highlighted (ERASE in Figure 3.3). John could move the highlighting to any option, and press RETURN when the one he wanted was highlighted. He chose ERASE. The computer told him to move the cursor to the beginning of the text to erase and press the RETURN key. John did so,

FIGURE 3.3   The word processing program in edit mode.

and the computer instructed him to move the cursor to the end of the text to be erased and again press RETURN. As John used the cursor control keys, the computer highlighted the words that would be erased (see Figure 3.4). When John pressed RETURN, the highlighted words disappeared and the words following them moved to close the space.

Next, John noticed he had used the word *ever* in many of his sentences, but that it wasn't necessary. Remembering that his teacher told him to "omit needless words," he decided to replace all the extraneous uses of *ever* with just a space. To do so, he selected the REPLACE option on the edit menu. The computer prompted him to enter the word or phrase he wanted to replace, and what he wanted to replace it with. John instructed the computer to leave just a space wherever the word *ever* appeared. The computer then highlighted each occurrence of *ever* in turn, and asked John to verify that he wanted to replace it. John pressed *Y* for yes each time. In this way, he was able to quickly replace all five occurrences of the word.

John then realized he left something out of the second paragraph. He said his parents had given him a program, but forgot to

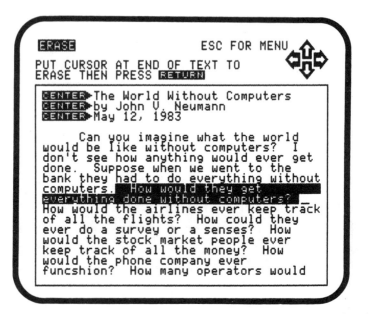

FIGURE 3.4   Marking the text to be erased.

say what the program did. He moved the cursor to after the sentence that ends with *Christmas* so he could add the missing information. He pressed ESC to return to write mode. Then, as John typed the words he wanted to add, the computer moved all the other words to make room. He entered:

> The program is for animations. It lets me make a picture on the screen and then make it move.

Next, John decided to remove the sentence about his attempt to write a program himself. He switched to edit mode and used the ERASE option as before. Figure 3.5 shows the second paragraph of John's essay after he made all these changes. John remarked that you would never know he had made all those changes, since the computer rearranged things as he changed them and it did not leave smudge marks where he had erased.

John then added another paragraph:

> My father uses computers in his work. He is a gardener. He uses a computer to keep track of his customers and his supplies. He types all the information into the computer.

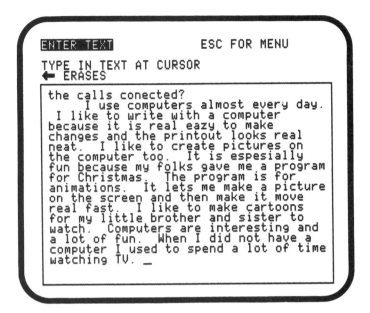

```
ENTER TEXT                  ESC FOR MENU
TYPE IN TEXT AT CURSOR
← ERASES
the calls conected?
      I use computers almost every day.
   I like to write with a computer
because it is real eazy to make
changes and the printout looks real
neat.  I like to create pictures on
the computer too.  It is espesially
fun because my folks gave me a program
for Christmas.  The program is for
animations.  It lets me make a picture
on the screen and then make it move
real fast.  I like to make cartoons
for my little brother and sister to
watch.  Computers are interesting and
a lot of fun.  When I did not have a
computer I used to spend a lot of time
watching TV. _
```

FIGURE 3.5   The word processing display after the second paragraph has been edited.

The computer printer writtes out the bills. He can get reports when he wants. That way he knows how much money people owe him and what he should order. Sometimes he even uses the computer to test out ideas about how plants should be aranged. Without a computer he would spend a lot more time working.

After writing this paragraph, John decided he should put it before the paragraph about his own use of computers. He pressed ESC for edit mode and selected the MOVE option. The computer instructed him to mark the beginning and end of the text he wanted to move (using the cursor control and RETURN keys, as he had done when erasing). It then prompted him to move the cursor to the new location for the text. He did so, pressed RETURN, and the paragraphs were rearranged almost instantly.

When John finished his essay, he entered *transfer mode*. Again, the computer displayed a menu of options. First, John wanted to save his essay on disk, in case he needed to change it later. He selected the SAVE option and the computer responded with:

NAME OF DISK FILE?

John could use any name he wanted. He typed:

Essay - May 12

The computer then saved his essay on a floppy disk. John could work on it again at any time by telling the computer to LOAD the file called ESSAY - MAY 12.

He then selected the PRINT option on the transfer menu. When he did so, the computer displayed the following information:

LEFT MARGIN...................COLUMN 10

RIGHT MARGIN.................COLUMN 70

SPACING....................................DOUBLE

LINES PER PAGE................................54

PAGE NUMBERING.........................NO

This showed the page formatting settings the computer would use if John did not make any changes. John wanted his essay single spaced, so he changed that setting. The format was then as John wanted, so he had the computer begin printing. The printer produced a copy of his essay in less than a minute.

John then quit the word processing program and loaded a spelling check program into the computer. When he ran the program it first asked him:

WHAT IS THE NAME OF THE DISK FILE TO CHECK?

John put the disk on which he had saved his essay into the disk drive and typed the name of his essay file:

Essay - May 12

The program then checked whether each word in John's essay matched a word in the program's dictionary, and it printed a list of the words for which no match was found. The spelling check program found most of John's misspellings: funcshion, conected, eazy, espesially writtes and aranged. Spelling check programs only test whether each word is contained in the computerized dictionary, not whether the word is used correctly. Therefore, the program did not catch John's use of *senses* when he meant *census*.

John likes being able to write down all his ideas before having to check his spelling, and then being able to correct misspelled words easily. Since the final printout always looks neat, he is proud of his work and wants to be sure all the words are spelled correctly. He also finds it helpful to be able to print a clean copy of his essay, read it carefully and then return to the computer to make changes.

John then loaded the word processing program again, so he could correct his essay and print a new copy. After he corrected his spelling errors and decided his essay was finished, he saved the corrected version on his disk, replacing the earlier version. He then instructed the computer to print two copies, one for himself and one for his teacher.

Ms. Byron pointed out that John is like many students, from second grade through college, who benefit from using computerized word processing. When they have to use paper and pen, these students are reluctant to write and unwilling to analyze and revise their essays. But when they use computerized word processing, they are enthusiastic about writing and put more effort into their essays. Ms. Byron added that she still regards learning to write by hand to be important. However, she believes word processing helps students develop skill in the thinking and creative aspects of writing. She added that word processing is especially beneficial for students whose writing is inhibited by slow or sloppy handwriting.

What about the need to type to use word processing? After some practice, many children and adults prefer typing to writing by hand. The ease of making corrections with the computer makes accurate typing less critical than it is with a standard typewriter. In addition, computers are ideal for presenting typing drill and practice (see Chapter 8), so they can be used to help teach the necessary skills. Ms. Byron added that typing and word processing are important skills for many jobs, and she is happy to see children mastering them in the early grades.

Teachers' Use of Word Processing

Teachers at Babbage School have found many ways to use word processing. Some use word processing programs to create tests and other materials for their classes. They can enter many questions, save them on a disk, and then select and print those desired for a particular test or lesson. Word processing is also ideal for making ditto masters. It is difficult to correct a ditto master after it is typed. But with word processing, the teacher can make all the corrections on the computer screen and then have the computer imprint the ditto master.

Some teachers have prepared stories with parts missing, or with errors in spelling, grammar and meaning. Students then use computerized word processing to complete or edit the work. In foreign language classes, students use word processing to prepare written translations and write stories in the foreign language. In other classes, students have prepared newsletters with word processing programs. Teachers report that word processing facilitates collaborative writing among students. Students working on the same story or article can independently make changes, print the revised version, and then compare their changes to those of their co-authors.

Ms. Byron noted that these are just some of the ways word processing can be used in education. Word processing is new to schools, and its many possible applications have just begun to be explored.

CREATING PICTURES WITH COMPUTERS

The field of *computer graphics*—creating and manipulating pictures with computers—has become important for many different functions. Computer generated pictures and animations are used in movies, television shows, advertising, and video games. Computer graphics are not limited by the laws of physics, so all kinds of special effects are possible. Any object can change color, appear and disappear, be transformed into other objects, move at incredible speeds, and perform other impossible actions.

Computer graphics are used in designing all sorts of things, from buildings and airplanes to clothing and toys. The design can be displayed on the computer screen, checked and revised, and subjected to simulated tests performed by the computer.

Another use of computer graphics is to create graphs and charts of financial reports, business trends, survey and election results, and other data. Computers can be programmed to automatically change an illustration as new data are entered. If a static picture is worth a thousand words, a picture that instantly changes as the data change is worth many thousands of words.

Graphics also play important roles in educational programs, such as those designed to teach geometry (e.g., illustrating the meaning of congruence), physics (e.g., showing how vectors combine) and geography (e.g., presenting lessons in map reading). More elaborate programs that have graphic representations of real scenes are used for such things as training pilots to land at different airports.

Computers also provide a new medium for artistic creativity. Just as word processing programs facilitate creating and revising writing, *graphics creation programs* facilitate creating and revising pictures. These programs let you create and modify a picture on the computer screen; change its size, shape, color and orientation; combine it with other pictures; and even animate it.

The Graphics Capabilities of Personal Computers

Computers vary widely in their graphics capabilities. Some are limited to black-and-white displays while others can produce multicolored displays. Computers with color capabilities vary in the number of colors and shades available. Computers also differ in the amount of detail possible in pictures. This is called the *resolution* of the display. You can think of the computer screen as a grid. Each location on the grid can be turned on or off, or, in color systems, set to a color. The number of locations on the grid determines the amount of detail that can be displayed.

High resolution graphics systems divide the screen into a large number of points, each of which can be controlled independently of the others. Typical personal computers with high resolution graphics have about 50,000 points on the screen (e.g., a grid with 250 points horizontally and 200 points vertically). *Low resolution graphics* systems divide the screen into blocks rather than points. Typical low resolution displays range from 960 blocks (48 by 20 grid) to 6144 blocks (128 by 48 grid). Figures 3.6 and 3.7 show outline maps of the United States created with high resolution and low resolution graphics.

Some low resolution systems let you use different shapes instead of just rectangular blocks. These shapes, called *graphics characters*, can be combined to form pictures. Typical sets of graphics characters include vertical, horizontal and diagonal lines; curves; boxes; circles; corners; and special shapes for computer games, such as hearts, diamonds, clubs and spades.

High resolution color graphics provides the most powerful system. Why then, isn't it always used? One reason is that color display screens are more expensive than black-and-white ones. Another reason is that high resolution and color require more memory than low resolution and black-and-white. Consider, for example, a black-and-white high resolution system with 50,000 points. The computer has to keep track of whether each point is on or off. To do so, one bit of memory is required for each point. If colors are added, more bits are required (the number of bits depends upon the number of colors available). Since high resolution and color require so much memory, low resolution and black-and-white are preferable when they can produce acceptable displays. Many personal com-

FIGURE 3.6   High resolution outline map of United States.

FIGURE 3.7   Low resolution outline map of United States.

puters provide several graphics modes so programmers can choose how much RAM memory to devote to graphics and how much to save for other parts of the program.

There are several ways to create pictures on a computer screen. Each programming language contains commands that instruct the computer to create graphics displays. In the next section, I describe how pictures can be created with a special set of *turtle graphics* commands available in some programming languages. Then I describe how pictures can be created directly on the computer screen, without writing a program.

Turtle Graphics

Turtle graphics is a set of commands used to instruct computers to create pictures. The name "turtle graphics" comes from an early computer system that controlled the movements of a robot shaped like a turtle. This computer could be used to program the turtle-robot to move and draw. In most current systems, the turtle is just a marker on the computer screen, but the same types of commands are used as with the turtle-robot. Simple commands tell the turtle to move forward or backward a number of steps, turn left or right a number of degrees, select a pen of a certain color, and raise or lower the pen to control whether the turtle leaves a trail as it moves.

Two children at Babbage School, Jason and Serena, showed me how they create pictures with turtle graphics. They loaded a program they had written into the computer and typed the word "MAGIC" followed by four numbers. Depending on the numbers typed, very different pictures appeared on the screen.

Serena typed MAGIC 5 90 10 8 and the turtle drew the picture shown in Figure 3.8. She explained that the program tells the turtle to draw a line, turn right a given number of degrees, draw a longer line, turn, draw an even longer line, turn, and so on for a number of repetitions. The first number after MAGIC is the length of the first line the turtle is to draw. The second number is the angle to turn. The third number is the amount to add to the length of each successive line. The fourth number is the number of turns to make before stopping. Therefore, when she typed MAGIC 5 90 10 8, the turtle drew a 5-step line, turned 90 degrees to the right, drew a 15-step line (the 5 of the prior line plus the 10 to be added to each successive line), turned 90 degrees, drew a 25-step line, and so on until 8 turns had been made.

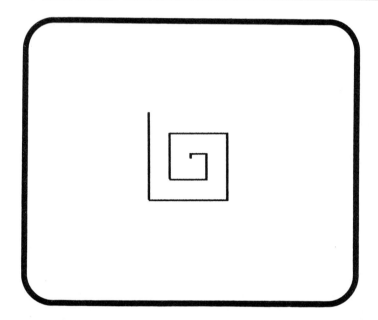

FIGURE 3.8   Picture created with the MAGIC program. The command was MAGIC 5 90 10 8.

5 = length of first line
90 = angle to turn between lines
10 = amount to increase length of each successive line
8 = number of times to turn before stopping

Figure 3.9 shows more interesting pictures Jason and Serena created with their MAGIC program, and the numbers they entered for each one. They instructed the computer to make a printed copy of each picture. When I asked to see the program, they listed it on the computer printer and pointed out that they called it MAGIC because while it can create many pictures, the whole program is only five lines long. Here is their program, written in the computer language called Logo:

```
TO MAGIC :START :ANGLE :INCREASE :TIMES
FORWARD :START RIGHT :ANGLE
IF :TIMES = 0 STOP
MAGIC (:START + :INCREASE) :ANGLE :INCREASE :TIMES −1
END
```

A. MAGIC 5 60 3 40

B. MAGIC 5 75 3 40

C. MAGIC 5 90 3 40

D. MAGIC 5 135 3 40

E. MAGIC 5 165 3 40

F. MAGIC 5 175 3 40

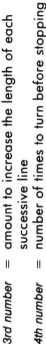

G. MAGIC 5 175 3 60

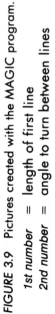

H. MAGIC 1 75 1 200

FIGURE 3.9 Pictures created with the MAGIC program.

1st number	=	length of first line
2nd number	=	angle to turn between lines
3rd number	=	amount to increase the length of each successive line
4th number	=	number of times to turn before stopping

43

These children enjoy creating pictures with their own programs and manipulating the commands and numbers to produce different patterns. Other students and many of the teachers prefer to create pictures with *graphics creation tools* instead of writing programs. Graphics creation tools are special programs and hardware that let you "draw" and "paint" directly on the computer screen.

Graphics Creation Tools

The children and teachers at Babbage School use several different types of graphics creation tools. All their programs require computers with high resolution color displays. Some of the programs also require special hardware devices.

Nine-year-old Sue demonstrated a graphics creation program that lets children use the computer keyboard and a joystick to make pictures. The joystick is the same type used for many computer games. Sue showed how she uses it to move a marker that serves as a "paint brush" on the screen. The program provides several options that are selected by pressing letters and numbers on the computer keyboard. Sue has a reference card that reminds her what each key does.

Sue pressed the *D* key to select the DRAW MODE. She then drew by moving the joystick in the direction she wanted the line to go, as if she were using a computerized Etch-A-Sketch. When she wanted to move her brush without leaving a line, she held down the button on the joystick. She changed the size of the brush and the color of the paint by pressing *B* (for brush) and then a number to set the brush size and a letter to select a color — *B* for blue, *R* for red, *G* for green and so on.

Other options in this program are for drawing lines, circles and rectangles. Sue demonstrated how these options are selected by pressing *L* for line, *C* for circle and *R* for rectangle. For each option, she used the joystick to move the marker to two points, pressing the button on the joystick each time to signal when the marker was at the desired location. In LINE MODE, the two points mark the ends of a line. In CIRCLE MODE the first point marks the center of the circle and the second point marks the circumference. In RECTANGLE MODE the two points mark the upper-left and lower-right corners. In each case, the computer automatically completed the figure after Sue marked the two points.

Sue especially enjoys the FILL MODE which lets her color areas of her picture. She selected a color and pressed *F* for fill. She moved the brush to the inside of a rectangle and pressed the joystick button. The computer quickly filled in the whole rectangle.

Another of Sue's favorites is RUBBER STAMP MODE. This lets her select a small picture and reproduce it anywhere on the screen. It can be a picture she previously created and saved on disk or part of her current picture. After she made a "rubber stamp," she used the joystick to locate the picture on the screen, pressing the joystick button each time she wanted to leave a copy.

Sue also demonstrated TEXT MODE, which is for adding letters and numbers to the picture. She can select from four sizes of letters, use the joystick to mark where she wants to place them, and then use the keyboard to type the letters.

Many of the children at Babbage School used this program to make Christmas cards last year. They enjoyed being able to make a set of pictures and then combine them in various ways to create different cards. Some children sent floppy disks containing many pictures to friends and relatives who have computers on which they could view them. The children also had their computer print copies of their pictures for people who did not have computers. However, the printed copies did not show the colors they had used on the computer screen. To be able to show the colors, some of the children took color photographs of their computer screen displays.

One of Sue's Christmas cards is shown in Figure 3.10. She used line mode to draw the tree, circle mode for the ornaments and rectangle mode for the presents. She used fill mode to color the ornaments and text mode to write HAPPY HOLIDAYS in large print. She carefully created one snowflake and duplicated it with rubber stamp mode. Finally, she used draw mode to add other lines and shadings, and then to sign her name.

Babbage School also has a special device, called a *graphics tablet*, which is used with a more elaborate graphics creation program. The graphics tablet is expensive and there is only one at the school, so its use is limited to children who have taken a special computer art class.

The graphics tablet is a thin, flat device, about eighteen inches on each side, with a stylus attached by a cable. Through a special interface and software, the computer can decode where on the tablet the stylus is pointed and whether the tip of the stylus is pressed against the tablet. Students and teachers can create a picture on the computer screen by moving the stylus on the graphics tablet. This is the closest thing in computer art to drawing with a real pen, pencil, or paint brush.

FIGURE 3.10 Christmas card created with a paint program.

The program used with the graphics tablet has all the features of the one used with the joystick, plus many additional ones. The computer artist can draw with the stylus, and the picture immediately appears on the computer screen. Special options in the program are used to create lines, circles, triangles and rectangles; fill areas with colors; duplicate images; and add lettering in many different styles and sizes. In addition, the artist can make the stylus work as if it were a paint brush of any size or shape, and he can draw with patterns as well as solid colors. Other options are used to relocate and rotate pictures on the screen.

One use of the graphics tablet is to transfer pictures from paper to the computer screen. The student or teacher places the drawing on the tablet and traces over it with the stylus. The program can be set to change the size of the picture as it is entered, so small pictures can be enlarged and large ones reduced.

Another option, called MAGNIFY, is used for detailed drawing. A section of the screen can be selected to be magnified. The computer will keep both the original and the magnified picture in memory, and the artist can switch which one is displayed on the screen. The artist can then change the magnified picture and, as

FIGURE 3.11   "Gene at the Tunnel" by Lucia Grossberger.

FIGURE 3.12   Gene's face magnified by a factor of four.

he does so, the computer automatically makes equivalent changes on the original drawing. This is like working on a section of the drawing under a magnifying glass. Figure 3.11 shows a drawing of a person, and Figure 3.12 shows a magnified view of the face.

Uses of Graphics Creation Tools

Students and teachers at Babbage School have found many uses for these sophisticated graphics creation tools. Two students use the computer to produce cartoons for the school newspaper. They have created pictures of a set of characters and objects and saved them on disk. They combine the pictures and add to the drawing as needed to create their cartoons. They can adjust the size and orientation of each part of the picture until they are satisfied with the overall effect. They can add letters anywhere in the picture, selecting from a wide variety of sizes and styles. When finished, they send a printed copy and a copy on disk to the editor of the school newspaper. The disk is useful for the editor in case she wants to change the size of the cartoon before printing it in the newspaper. Figure 3.13 shows one of the cartoons.

FIGURE 3.13   Cartoon created with computer and graphics tablet.

Other students have created all sorts of pictures, ranging from abstracts to portraits, with the graphics programs and hardware.

Some teachers use the graphics system in creating their own computer programs. For example, one teacher has created a series of biology lessons. He used the graphics tablet to transfer pictures from a book to the computer, and then used a special program to combine the pictures with written information and questions. By having the computer rapidly display sequences of pictures, he created animations illustrating how the heart pumps blood. Another teacher has created displays of constellations for science lessons, using sequences of pictures that show how the star patterns change. He shows them on a large display screen while he presents the lessons.

The variety of graphics creation tools at Babbage School makes computer art accessible to every student and teacher. Graphics is certainly one of the most widely used and enjoyed applications of computers at the school. I asked the art teacher why children should learn about computer art and she gave me the following quotation from Alex Packer, author of a book called *Paint* that accompanies a graphics creation program:

> It only seems appropriate that a culture so thoroughly linked to technology and machines should create art with the ultimate machine of our times, the computer. The computer is an artist's tool. Instead of a chisel, a brush, a stick or a trowel, the artist paints with a computer. Instead of oil paints, acrylics, pastels, charcoal or sand, the artist paints with electronics. Instead of canvas, plaster, wood, marble or paper, the artist paints on a cathode ray tube; light is the medium. Throughout history, the breakthroughs of science have been integrated, directly and symbolically, with art forms.... Where will it lead? Nobody knows. It will take years to explore the expanded creative flexibility and techniques offered by the computer.*

COMPUTERS AND MUSIC

Music and sound effects produced with computers have advanced a long way since the "pings" and "pongs" that introduced computer sounds to many people. In addition to the sounds of video games,

---

* Alex Packer, *Paint* (Reston, VA: Reston Publishing Company) pp. 102–103. Copyright 1982 by the Capital Children's Museum, Washington, D.C.

computers are used to produce music and sound effects for movies, record albums and live performances. Computers can imitate the sounds of any instrument, as well as produce novel sounds. They can alter the pitch, tempo and timber of music, and manipulate sounds in other ways. These capabilities make computers powerful new creative tools for composers and musicians.

Many personal computers can produce sounds and tones, either through a small built-in speaker or by being connected to a television or stereo system. The sound capabilities of personal computers vary. For example, some computers can produce only one note at a time, so chords cannot be played. Others can produce four or more notes at a time, over a wide range of octaves. Computers with these more sophisticated sound capabilities can also be programmed to produce elaborate sound effects.

In addition to the built-in sound capabilities, special music devices have been connected to personal computers. Combined with special software, these devices give personal computers the capability to produce all sorts of music and sound effects. Special music input devices have also been developed, since computer keyboards are not well suited for entering music. For example, one special music input device is like an electric organ keyboard.

Computers have many potential applications in music education. Teachers have used computers to demonstrate the sounds of different instruments and styles of music, and to show the effects of changing the key or tempo of different pieces. Computers can provide automated drill and practice for ear training and sight reading. Computers are also used to help students learn to play songs. A musical score is entered into the computer. The computer then plays the music at a slow speed while displaying the notes, and the student plays along on his instrument. As the student masters the piece, the computer is instructed to increase the speed of its accompaniment.

With *music editing programs*, students can compose music or enter already created music into a computer. Music editing programs are similar in operation to word processing programs, but they work with notes instead of letters. You can enter the notes either by typing on the keyboard or using a special input device. The computer displays and plays each note. You can delete, insert, or rearrange the notes; have the computer play them; save them on disk; and, in some systems, have the computer print the score. Music editing programs thereby provide an effective way for students to compose their own music and explore different note patterns, tempos and other variations. This can be done without any musical instruments, so new musical experiences are made accessible to students who have not learned to play an instrument.

Babbage School does not have any sophisticated computer music systems, but the children enjoy and learn from a simple program. The program works on a computer with a built-in speaker and does not require any special hardware. It turns the computer into an instrument with a three-octave range. Only one note can be played at a time, so chords are not possible.

The program begins by asking the student to specify the meter, key signature and tempo of the music to be entered. A staff appears on the screen and the program turns the computer keyboard into a miniature piano. The middle row of keys represents the notes. The letter *A* is the note *C*, the letter *S* is the note *D*, and so on. The keys above and below are for sharps and flats, and the space bar is used for rests. Special labels are put on the letters to remind students which one represents each note.

When the child presses a key, the note appears on the staff and the sound is played. The length of the note is determined by how long the key is held down. The student presses the RETURN key at the end of each measure, and the computer checks whether the measure contains an acceptable combination of note durations. For example, if 3/4 time was set and the student enters three half notes, the computer will warn that the timing of the measure is incorrect and prompt the student to enter notes of the appropriate length.

After students enter music, they can change it using cursor control keys and INSERT, DELETE and MOVE commands similar to those used in the word processing program. They also use a REPEAT command for segments of music they want to use more than once. They can have the computer play the music at any time, and they can explore changing the tempo and pitch. Music can be saved on disk, and the computer can print copies of the score. Some students enjoy making tape recordings of their computer music.

This program, although not very sophisticated, encourages students to explore music, trying different combinations of notes, tempos and keys. Many students enter songs they know and then experiment with revising them in various ways. This helps them learn the principles of music and composition. The music program has led some students to a better appreciation of music and has contributed to their interest in learning to play instruments.

Chapter 4

Gathering, Organizing and Analyzing Information

We have entered the Information Age. For the first time in history, more people's jobs involve working with information than with goods. As a result, information processing machines—computers—have become the primary tools of our time.

The teachers at Babbage School aim to prepare students to be successful in the Information Age. They emphasize that every student should develop skill at gathering, organizing, analyzing and communicating information. Furthermore, they regard learning to use computer tools for processing information to be as important as learning to use the library.

A central tenet at Babbage School is that students learn best by doing. Beginning in the fifth grade, students do research projects. While working on their projects, they learn about their specific topics and, more importantly, they learn how to gather, organize and interpret information. Students prepare both written and spoken presentations of their research, so they also develop communication skills. These projects are considered to be among the most valuable learning experiences at Babbage School. One student explained why it is so important to learn how to do research: "There's too much stuff to know to keep it all in your head, and it changes all the time. If you're smart, you know how to find out what you need to know, when you need to know it."

While working on their projects, students learn to use computers in diverse ways. They use large data base systems to locate needed information, and computer communication systems to get information from people in other places. They use computerized filing systems to store and organize information, and programs to do calculations and perform other analyses. They use word processing programs to prepare written reports, and graphics programs to create charts, graphs and other pictorial displays. These computer tools enable students to work with more information, perform more detailed and sophisticated analyses, and prepare better reports than would be possible otherwise.

GATHERING INFORMATION

In Mr. Marconi's seventh-grade social studies class, groups of students collaborate on research projects. Mr. Marconi encourages students to work together to plan their research, find and understand relevant material, and prepare presentations of their findings. He also makes sure to allow sufficient time for students to tackle large projects, do in-depth research, and carefully consider the material before preparing their presentations.

Mr. Marconi provides his students with a great deal of support and guidance. Once the students have selected their topics, he helps them gather relevant information. He particularly encourages them to find up-to-date material from newspapers, books and journals, and he teaches them to use computerized information bases to locate information.

Babbage School subscribes to a computerized information retrieval system called *Dialog*SM. Dialog is an enormous storehouse of information, organized into almost 200 different data bases. There are data bases covering education, psychology, science, computers, business, law, current events, government publications, books, magazines, software, biographies, patents, dissertations, and numerous other topics. With a few simple commands, students can have the Dialog computer list references for articles about whatever topics they choose.

Three students, Robert, Joan and Tripper, were interested in doing a project on energy conservation. Mr. Marconi suggested they select a specific area of conservation, and they agreed upon automobile transportation and gasoline conservation.

Robert, Joan and Tripper wanted to use the Dialog information system to find relevant articles. Mr. Marconi gave them the Dialog Users Manual and an account number and password. He explained that the cost to the school depends upon how much time students are connected to the Dialog system, and that there is a limited budget. To keep the time they use Dialog to a minimum, students are expected to be well organized and know in advance which data bases they will use and how they will go about searching for relevant information.

The students looked through the list of data bases to decide which ones would be likely to contain information about automobiles and gasoline conservation. Since they were looking for up-to-date, non-technical information, they agreed to begin with the data bases covering newspapers and magazines. They found two that seemed ideal. One was *The National Newspaper Index*, which contains all articles, news reports, editorials, columns and reviews found in five major newspapers: *New York Times, Washington Post, Los Angeles Times, Christian Science Monitor*, and *Wall Street Journal*. The information goes back to 1979 and is updated every month. The second index they chose was the *Magazine Index*, which contains references to the contents of over 370 popular American magazines. This index goes back to 1973, and about 12,000 new references are added every month.

Joan pointed out that there are also data bases that focus specifically on energy. She selected three she thought would be useful: the *Department of Energy Index*, which contains references and summaries of all the unclassified information processed at the Technical Information Center of the United States Department of Energy; *Energyline*, which covers both technical and non-technical articles; and *Energynet*, which lists people and organizations working on energy-related issues. Robert and Tripper were concerned that the articles in the Department of Energy Index would be too technical for them to understand, and that using all these indices would give them more information than they could handle. They therefore decided to check the newspaper and magazine indices first, and then use the other ones only if they needed more information.

The next step was for Joan, Robert and Tripper to decide how to best obtain information relevant to their topic from the data bases they had selected. They read about the Dialog system and learned that the information about each article is grouped into what is called a *record*. For example, a record in the National Newspaper Index contains the title of the article, the author, the newspaper in which it appeared, the date and page number, a list of the people named in the article, and a list of *descriptor* words and phrases that describe the contents of the article. The students can have the computer select all the articles that have a specific word in their records (e.g., all the articles with *energy*) or a combination of words (e.g., all the articles with both *energy* and *automobile*) They can even have the computer leave out articles with certain words (e.g., select all the articles with *energy* and *automobile* but not *gasohol*). They can also limit the articles selected to particular newspapers or magazines, authors, and years.

Joan, Robert and Tripper agreed that their first search word should be *automobile*. Robert pointed out that some articles might use the word *car* instead, so they should have the computer search for both terms. They chose *energy* and *conservation* as other important search words, and planned to have the computer select only those articles that have both these terms, as well as *automobile* or *car*, in their records. If these search words gave them too many articles, they planned to have the computer select those published within the last two years.

To retrieve information from the Dialog system, students connect a computer in their school to the large Dialog computer. Their school's computer has a special device called a *modem*, which enables it to transmit information via standard telephone lines. The students also use a *terminal program*, which gives their computer instructions for sending and receiving information. The program lets them quickly *download* information from the Dialog computer to their own, save it on a disk, and then print and read it later. This saves money, since it reduces the time they spend connected to the Dialog computer.

Tripper plugged the modem into a telephone jack, loaded the program, and then, in response to a set of choices shown on the computer screen, told the computer they wanted to use the Dialog system. The computer automatically dialed the number by playing the correct tones into the phone. (A special computer communication network makes it possible to connect to Dialog with a local phone call from most places in the United States.)

The Dialog computer responded by asking for an account number and password. After typing the number and password Mr. Marconi had given them, Tripper typed the command that tells the computer they want to use the National Newspaper Index, which happens to be index number 111:

BEGIN 111

The computer acknowledged the command by responding with the date, time and name of the data base:

4/21/83   15:29:45 EST
Now in National Newspaper Index Database
(Copyright 1983 Information Access Corp.)

First, the students wanted to select all those references about automobiles. They therefore instructed the Dialog computer to:

FIND AUTOMOBILE OR CAR

This told the computer to find all the references in the data base that have the word *automobile* or *car* in the title or list of descriptive terms. The computer responded with:

        11929 Automobile
        2391 Car
S1   12726 Automobile and car

This means 11,929 references contain the word *automobile* and 2,391 contain the word *car*. There are 12,726 different records containing *automobile* or *car* (or both terms—articles that contain both are only counted once). The computer labeled this set of records S1, for set number 1.

The students then entered their other keywords and the computer responded to each:

FIND GASOLINE

S2   2638   Gasoline

FIND CONSERVATION

S3   2123   Conservation

The computer's responses show that set 2 contains 2,638 records with the word *gasoline* and set 3 contains 2,123 records with the word *conservation*. Joan, Robert and Tripper wanted to know how many records in the data base are about automobiles, gasoline and conservation. That is, they wanted to select those references that are in all three sets. They therefore gave the following command:

COMBINE S1 AND S2 AND S3

The computer responded:

S4   17   S1 S2 and S3

That is, there are seventeen references about automobiles and gasoline conservation.

They then had the Dialog computer give the title for each article and the information they would need to find the original publication. To do so, they entered the command:

DISPLAY S4/3/1-17

This tells the computer to display records 1 through 17 of set number 4. The 3 in the middle is a code number that tells the computer to display the title, newspaper and date of the article. Other code numbers would limit the display to just the titles, or expand it to include all the descriptor terms. The computer responded with all the information. The students had their computer rapidly accept and save all the information on a disk, so they could print and carefully check it after they disconnected from the Dialog computer.

Next, the students told the Dialog system they wanted to use the Magazine Index. They entered the same commands and search words, and the computer reported that there were twenty-four relevant references in this data base. As before, they had their computer rapidly accept and store the information on a disk. They then used a LOGOFF command to tell the Dialog computer they were finished. The final information Dialog displayed showed they had been connected to the Dialog computer for less than 10 minutes and the total bill for their work was $3.92.

ORGANIZING INFORMATION

After disconnecting from the Dialog system, Joan, Robert and Tripper had their classroom computer system print three copies of the seventeen newspaper and twenty-four magazine references they had obtained. Each person read through the list and checked the articles he or she was interested in reading.

They decided to use an *information filing* program to keep track of the articles, who read each one, and the summaries they would prepare. As in the Dialog system, the information about each article in the students' filing system is grouped together into a record. Each specific piece of information within a record, such as the title of the article or the author, is called a *field* of information. The records are stored on a disk that can be duplicated easily, so each student can have his or her own copy of the files.

The filing program makes it easy for the students to enter records, organize them, find what they need, and change records, while maintaining a neat and organized filing system. The program can sort records into alphabetic or numerical order according to any single field. It can perform simple analyses, such as counting the number of records that contain a given keyword or calculating the averages of numbers in certain fields. It can also print copies of the records and analyses.

The students' first step in using the filing program was to decide what information should go in each record. They definitely wanted to include the information they had obtained from Dialog: the title, author, newspaper or magazine, date, and page number of each article. In addition, they had decided to divide the work by having each person read some of the articles and prepare summaries for the others. They therefore added a field for the name of the person who read the article and a field for the summary. They had to tell the filing program how much space to reserve for each field, so they agreed to limit the summaries to 250 words. Tripper was concerned that the work would not be divided evenly, since some articles would be longer than others. They therefore added a field for the number of pages in the article. They could then have the computer calculate the number of pages each person had read.

The students made the following list of the fields of information they would have in each record:

1. Title of article
2. Author
3. Newspaper or magazine
4. Date
5. Page number
6. Who read it
7. Summary
8. Number of pages

Then they entered the information they had obtained from Dialog into the first five fields. Later, as they worked on their summaries, they would add the information for the last three fields.

At this point, some of their 41 records were:

The other side of cheaper fuel
Schuon, Marshall
New York Times
Feb 27, 1983
Section 2, page 24

GM, Ford missing fuel-economy target
Simison, Robert L.
Wall Street Journal
Feb 7, 1983
page 8

Ways to save gas
Garretson, Kim
Better Homes and Gardens
July 1982
page 12

Are lower oil prices good news or bad?
No author listed
U.S. News and World Report
April 5, 1982
page 42

Don't fall for these gas-saving schemes
Berman, Clifford
Good Housekeeping
Sept 1981
page 236

Gasoline use creeps up
No author listed
New York Times
June 21, 1981
Section 3, page 18

The search for the magic gas-saver
U.S. News and World Report
No author listed
May 25, 1981
page 84

Promises that are full of gas (fuel-saving devices)
Bruman, Carol
Macleans
Jan 5, 1981
page 44

30 things you should know to beat the high
costs of gas
Candler, Julie
Woman's Day
Aug 5, 1980
page 46

Cars consume more gas during warmup
No author listed
Design News
May 5, 1980
page 33

Fifty fuel savers
Nerpel, Chuck
Motor Trend
Aug 1979
page 22

More gasoline-saving tips for the motorist
No author listed
New York Times
July 15, 1979
Section 10, page 3

Joan volunteered to check all the *New York Times* articles, since she knew they were available on microfilm at the local library. With one command, she had the computer retrieve the records for all the *New York Times* articles in their file. She added her name in the appropriate field of each one and had the computer print copies of all these records. Robert and Tripper chose the articles that interested them, added their names to the records, and had the computer print a list for each of them. Then they had the computer print a list of all the articles no one had chosen yet. They decided to keep these for later, until they knew whether the library had all the articles they wanted, and how many pages of articles each of them had chosen so far.

DEVELOPING A SURVEY AND ANALYZING THE RESPONSES

Joan, Robert and Tripper spent three weeks reading articles, entering their summaries into the filing system, and going over each other's summaries. They found many ways in which gasoline could be conserved, and they decided to find out how much gasoline their schoolmates' families could save. With Mr. Marconi's help, they developed a questionnaire to obtain information about how much people drive and whether their cars and driving habits are energy efficient.

The students used a word processing program to develop the questionnaire. This made it easy for them to make additions and deletions as they debated what should be included. It also helped them arrange the final questionnaire into a neat, organized format. Their questionnaire is shown in Table 4.1.

Joan, Robert and Tripper gave copies of the questionnaire to all their classmates to see if their parents would answer the questions. They also sent copies to some of their friends in other schools. As the responses began to come in, they got together to decide how to analyze the information they were collecting.

Robert's father had taught him how to use a program called *VisiCalc®*,* and Robert thought it would help them analyze their survey data. VisiCalc® is a *spreadsheet* program. This means it is like having a large sheet of paper on which you create a table. However, the computer spreadsheet has important advantages over a paper one. The computer spreadsheet can shrink and enlarge as your work progresses, so you are not limited to one particular size. You can easily delete, add, or move columns and rows, without having to resort to the scissors and tape that would be needed with a paper spreadsheet. Most importantly, the computer can be instructed to automatically perform calculations and fill in parts of the table.

Robert explained to Joan and Tripper how they could use Visi-Calc®. He showed them that an empty spreadsheet has numbers marking the rows and letters marking the columns. The top of the screen has an area for the computer to display questions and prompts, and for you to enter responses and commands. Robert demonstrated how a large marker shows the current row and column, and how you can move the marker by pressing certain keys. If you have a large spreadsheet, the computer screen can only show a small part of it at a time, but as you move the marker the screen shows different sections of the spreadsheet. To see the whole thing at once, you have the computer print a copy.

Robert explained that you can put a label, a number or a formula into each box. If you use a formula, the computer automati-

* VisiCalc® is a registered trademark of Personal Software, Inc., VisiCorp.

TABLE 4.1
Joan, Robert and Tripper's Questionnaire

Automobile Questionnaire

. GENERAL INFORMATION

. Name:
. Type of car:
. Year car made:
. Miles per gallon in city driving:
. Miles per gallon in highway driving:

. ACTUAL RECORDS FOR ONE WEEK

ease fill in this table with the records you kept for one week:

rpose of Driving	City Miles	Highway Miles
iving to work		
opping/chores		
her driving		
tals		

POSSIBLE MILEAGE SAVINGS

ease fill in how much you think you could reduce the number of
les you drive each week.

iving Reduced By	City Miles Saved	Highway Miles Saved
r pooling		
mbining or cutting trips		
lking or bicycling		
king a bus or train		

POSSIBLE MILES PER GALLON SAVINGS

w many months since your last tune up?
you have radial tires?
w fast do you drive on average on the highway?

cally does the calculations for you. Robert showed how they could
arrange their own spreadsheet by placing labels on it. First, they
wanted to enter each person's data for city miles driven, highway
miles driven, miles per gallon for city driving, and miles per gallon
for highway driving. Robert entered appropriate labels at the tops
of columns A, B, C and D (see Figure 4.1). Then he had the

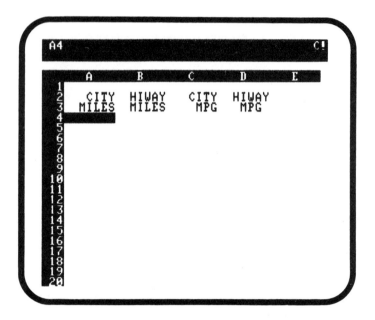

FIGURE 4.1 VisiCalc® program display after the column headings have been entered. The marker is at box A4.

computer draw a line to neatly separate the labels from the data, and he entered the data from the first ten questionnaires that had been returned.

Finally, Robert explained the "real neat part of VisiCalc®." He added the label GAS USED to the top of the next column, E. He then moved the cursor to the top row of data, so it was in box E5. He entered a formula that told the computer how to calculate the total number of gallons of gas used from the information in the other columns. The formula told the computer to divide the number of city miles driven (box A5) by the city miles-per-gallon (C5) and add the result to the number of highway miles driven (B5) divided by the highway miles-per-gallon (D5). The computer instantly did the calculation and displayed the answer in box E5 (see Figure 4.2). Robert then entered a short sequence of commands that told the computer to repeat this calculation for all the other rows. It immediately displayed the correct numbers in column E (see Figure 4.3).

Robert also showed that after he entered the formulas he could change an entry in column A, B, C or D and the computer would

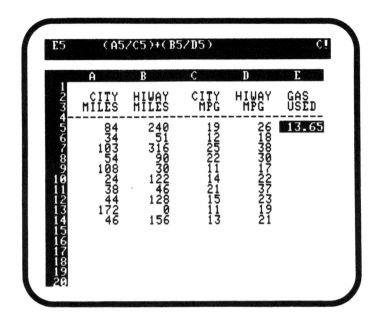

FIGURE 4.2   VisiCalc® program display after the formula for box
E5 has been entered. The formula is shown at the top of the screen.

automatically recalculate the corresponding number in column E.
Tripper thought this was fantastic, since it would save so much
work. He could correct mistakes in entering data without having
to redo the calculations. Robert explained that not only is it good
for fixing mistakes, but it also lets you change numbers to explore
different possibilities. His father calls this "making projections."
Robert then went on to demonstrate special commands for finding
totals, averages, and minimum and maximum values of rows or
columns.

Joan pointed out that it would have been a good idea to put
the name of the person who provided the data in the first column
of each row. Robert quickly instructed the computer to shift all
the information over one column, added the label NAME to the
first column, and entered each name on the appropriate line. The
students then added columns for the other information they had
collected with their questionnaire and entered all the responses
they had received.

They easily instructed the computer to calculate how much
gasoline each person could save by reducing the number of miles

E5	(A5/C5)+(B5/D5)			C!
A	**B**	**C**	**D**	**E**

	A	B	C	D	E
1					
2	CITY	HIWAY	CITY	HIWAY	GAS
3	MILES	MILES	MPG	MPG	USED
4	-----	-----	-----	-----	-----
5	84	240	19	26	13.65
6	34	51	12	18	5.67
7	103	316	25	38	12.44
8	54	90	22	30	5.45
9	108	30	11	17	11.58
10	24	122	14	22	7.26
11	38	46	21	37	3.05
12	44	128	15	23	8.50
13	172	0	11	19	15.64
14	46	156	13	21	10.97
15					
16					
17					
18					
19					
20					

FIGURE 4.3 VisiCalc® program display after the computer has been instructed to replicate the formula for all rows of data.

he or she drives. They then considered the possible savings from getting the cars tuned, using radial tires, and changing driving habits. They had read that a car uses about 1 percent more gasoline for each month since its last tune-up, that radial tires give 2.5 percent better mileage than other tires, and that you use 1 percent more gas for each mile-per-hour faster than 50 you drive. They used these numbers to work out the formulas for the computer to calculate how much gasoline could be saved. Then they printed reports that told each person who had completed the questionnaire how much gasoline he or she could conserve.

The students had the computer add the amount of gasoline that could be saved in all the various ways, and they showed their analysis to Mr. Marconi. He thought they had done an excellent job, but wasn't sure about the formula they had used to combine all the information into the total possible savings for each individual. The students checked their formula and changed it. As Tripper pointed out, all they had to do was give the computer the new formula and it instantly did all the calculations for them.

Joan, Robert and Tripper discussed their project with Mr. Marconi. They agreed upon three more things to do before they would begin using the word processor to write their report. One was to use Visicalc to work out some "what-if" projections, such as "What if everyone bought a car that got 50 miles to the gallon?" and "What if computers made it possible for people to work at home half the time, thereby cutting the amount they drive to work in half?"

The second thing was to use a special program to create graphs and pictures from the data they had collected. The program can produce bar charts, line graphs, pie graphs, and other pictorial displays of data. The students planned to make one graph showing the percentages of miles actually driven for work, chores and recreation, and another graph showing how much driving could be reduced by car pooling, using buses, and other means.

The third thing Mr. Marconi suggested was the most interesting to the students. They would compare the possibilities for conserving gasoline for people who live in city, surburban and rural areas. All they needed to do was to get enough people from these areas to fill out their questionnaire. They decided to try using a computer communication system called the *Source*SM. Like Dialog, they could connect to the large Source computer from a computer in their own school. Many people use the Source. It lets them leave messages for each other, place notices on computerized "bulletin boards," organize "conferences" for people interested in a common topic, and even "chat" with other people who are connected to the Source computer at the same time.

The students placed an announcement on the computerized bulletin board. They also found that there was a Source conference about ecology, and they left a special announcement for all the people who took part in it. The announcement said that a group of seventh-grade students needed people to complete a questionnaire about gasoline conservation for a class project. Anyone interested was asked to leave a message for the students on the Source, and they would send, via the Source electronic mail service, a copy of the questionnaire. The person could use a word processing program available on the Source to complete the questionnaire and return the answers via the electronic mail service. The entire communication could take place on computer screens, without any paper being used.

The first person who completed their survey was a woman in London, England who used the Source from her home. The students realized that with the computer communication system they might even be able to compare different countries. They planned to check with their teachers about translating the questionnaire into French and Spanish.

The students were excited about this new possibility. Tripper pointed out that without the computer communication system, they would never be able to collect enough data from different places. He realized how much the computers had helped with their project, and said that without computers they would probably still be in the library looking for references. Robert disagreed, saying they would probably be sitting around with their calculators trying to do all the work they were able to do in a few minutes with VisiCalc®. Certainly, the computer made many aspects of their research easier, and it opened entirely new possibilities for them to explore. They were excited about their project and eager to present a report of their findings to their classmates.

Chapter 5

Learning By Exploring Computer Simulations

A sign in a classroom at Babbage School reads:

I HEAR AND I FORGET.

I SEE AND I REMEMBER.

I DO AND I UNDERSTAND.

Learning is generally most successful and enjoyable when it is the result of active exploration, discovery and play, rather than more passive watching, listening and reading. Exploration and play provide opportunities for *experiential learning* which is motivated and guided by the learner's own curiosity and interests. In experiential learning, students actively explore objects and situations, and they learn from discovering the results of their actions.

Active learners have a great deal of control over what they learn and how they go about learning it. However, it is not enough for children to be active. They must also be able to observe and understand the effects of their actions. That is, a responsive environment is necessary for experiential learning to be successful. The role of teachers is to provide appropriate materials for students to explore, and to provide guidance and assistance.

A preschool child playing with building blocks provides a good example of how children learn naturally through playful exploration. The child combines blocks of various shapes to create a structure. He may have an idea of the structure he wants to build or he may develop his ideas as he stacks the blocks. As the child builds, he can immediately see the results of his actions. If the blocks fall or do not look as the child intended, he will rearrange them. While working with blocks, the child may learn about size relationships and balance, discovering, for example, the advantages of placing small blocks atop larger ones.

Many educators have emphasized the virtues of learning by doing. John Dewey, an American philosopher who was one of the most influential advocates of experiential learning, wrote:

> The fundamental fallacy in [standard] methods of instruction ... consists in supposing that we can begin with the ready-made subject matter of arithmetic, or geography, or whatever, irrespective of some direct personal experience.... The first stage of contact with any new material, at whatever age of maturity, must inevitably be of the trial and error sort. An individual must actually try, in play or work, to do something with material ... and then note the interaction of his energy and that of the material employed. This is what happens when a child at first begins to build with blocks, and it is equally what happens when a scientific man in his laboratory begins to experiment with unfamiliar objects.... [Effective methods of instruction] give the pupils something to do, not something to learn; and the doing is of such a nature as to demand thinking, or the intentional noting of connections.*

Experiential learning is common in informal learning situations, and it is employed at every level of formal education. Educational toys and school science laboratories are designed to encourage active learning. Through experiential learning, students acquire new knowledge, master skills, test ideas, gain understanding of general principles, and develop thinking and communication abilities.

The interactive nature of personal computers makes them ideal vehicles for active learning experiences akin to children building with blocks or scientists testing hypotheses. As I described in the previous chapter, computers can facilitate active exploration of a wide variety of creative possibilities in writing, music or art. In this chapter, I focus on how computers can encourage active learning through simulations that allow students to explore situations created within the computer.

* John Dewey, *Democracy and Education* (New York: MacMillan Company, 1916) p. 180.

COMPUTER SIMULATIONS

Active learning is usually limited by the number of objects, places and experiences available for students to explore. But suppose we could make almost any type of experience available to students. They could learn about zero gravity environments by spending an hour in one. They could learn about city government by becoming the mayor and members of the city council. They could perform genetic engineering experiments with DNA, no matter how dangerous and infeasible such experiments would be in a real laboratory. They could experience being businessmen, airline pilots, architects, real estate brokers, generals, explorers, archeologists and astronauts. These are just some of the wide variety of roles and situations students can learn about through computer simulations.

A simulation is a dynamic representation of a real object, situation or environment. A representation reflects the main properties of an actual object or event as, for example, a map represents a city. A map, however, is static—it does not change in response to any type of action. A simulation is a *dynamic* representation because it responds and changes in a manner analogous to the real object, situation or environment. Students can explore simulations and learn from experiencing how the simulations respond to their actions.

Some simulations, such as the board game *Monopoly*, are familiar to almost everyone. Monopoly simulates a real estate market. Each player assumes the role of an investor who buys, sells and trades properties, trying to gain good locations to build houses and hotels, and thereby amass a fortune.

Children can learn a great deal from playing Monopoly. The game involves rents, taxes, utility bills and banking, as well as financial successes and failures. Players must decide how to spend a limited amount of money wisely, and they learn about making investments for future rewards. They practice negotiation skills, which can be developed only through experience. Many aspects of the game involve reading and math skills. For example, children might learn about percentages as a result of landing on the dreaded income tax square and having to pay ten percent of their assets.

The aim of a simulation is to capture the main characteristics of what is being represented. Simulations are never complete and precise representations. The precision and completeness required depends upon the purposes for which the simulation will be used. For example, Monopoly is an ample simulation for children to learn about handling money and investing, but much more realistic and detailed simulations are required when computers are used to help train airline pilots.

Computer simulations have advantages over other types of simulations. They can capture more aspects of reality and give people more flexibility in how they explore and experience the simulated environment. In a computer simulation, time and space can be compacted or expanded; dangerous, expensive and impossible actions can be attempted; graphics, animations and sound can provide information and make the simulation more realistic; and situations can be repeated and varied at will. Computer simulations are powerful tools that expand the opportunities for active learning.

A ROAD TRIP SIMULATION

One simulation program used at Babbage School is called *Roadtrip*. Roadtrip is a simple simulation, suitable for children in the early grades.

Like many simulations, Roadtrip takes the form of a game. The aim of the game is to complete a trip to Greenstone Park as rapidly and inexpensively as possible. Along the way, children learn about many of the events that can occur while traveling by car, such as stopping at hotels, gas stations and restaurants; getting lost; and encountering hitch-hikers, speed traps, flat tires and detours. This game is usually played by one child at a time, but sometimes young children play together to help each other with the reading and decisions.

Sue, a student in the fourth grade, had never played Roadtrip before. Since her friends and teacher recommended it, she decided to give it a try. The program started by asking whether she would like instructions. The instructions told her that the goal of the game is to get to Greenstone Park within two days while spending no more than $200. The instructions also told her the main commands she could use to drive her car and get information. These were:

F = drive forward
R = drive to the right
L = drive to the left
T = turn around
S = change the speed
$\$$ = check how much money is left
M = check the map

At various points in the trip, the computer displayed other choices on the screen. Sue could make a selection by pressing the first letter of the choice she wanted.

The simulation started with the display shown in Figure 5.1. The traveler was already in her car. The speedometer on the dashboard showed she was traveling at thirty miles per hour, the odometer showed forty-seven miles, the gas gauge read about three-quarters full, the alternator and oil warning lights were off, and the time was 5:44. The rear view mirror near the top of the display showed the road behind the car. The sun was shining and there were a few clouds. All that was visible in the distance was the road curving to the left, a sign and a few trees. Sue pressed L to follow the road to the left.

The next display showed that Sue had reached the town of Dullsville (see Figure 5.2). The choices on the screen told her that she could purchase gas, register at the hotel, eat or continue. She first purchased gas, finding that gas in Dullsville cost $1.96 per gallon. Fortunately, she only needed four gallons to fill her tank. She decided to eat, and spent $4.50 in the Dullsville cafe for orange

FIGURE 5.1 Starting the road trip.

You are in DULLSVILLE.
The time is 6:24.
You may purchase gas, register at the
hotel, eat, or continue. Your choice? ■

FIGURE 5.2   Arriving at Dullsville.

juice, a cheese omelet, toast and milk. She then decided to continue
and took the road to the right.

Before continuing further, Sue pressed *M* to check her map and
the display shown in Figure 5.3 appeared on the computer screen.
She figured she must be on Route 11, since she took a right turn as
she left Dullsville. She planned to take Route 70, passing through
Oasis, Nevergreen and Lazy Hollow on her way to Greenstone Park.
Sue pressed $ to check her finances and found that she had $187.66
left, and she noted that the time was 8:40 AM. She set her speed to
65 miles per hour and continued down the road.

Sue ignored a 55 miles per hour speed limit sign and was soon
stopped by a policeman, fined $25.00 and delayed thirty minutes.
She set her speed back down to 55. She was delayed another thirty
minutes by a train, and passed a hitchhiker but decided not to stop
for him. Sue found the map lacked sufficient detail and took several
wrong turns near the cities. She wished she could get detailed maps
of each city, but they were not available in this simulation. She
missed the road to Oasis and, finding herself in Lake Woebegone,
decided to stop for gas and food. She was then sure she was on the
road to Nevergreen, but the road was a dead end (see Figure 5.4).
It was 7:41 PM (the stars in the sky showed it was night), so she
decided to return to Lake Woebegone and check into a hotel.

FIGURE 5.3 The map to Greenstone Park.

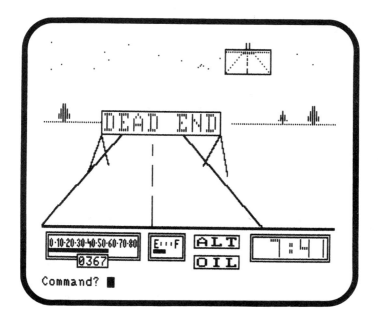

FIGURE 5.4 Reaching a dead end.

In the next day of the simulation Sue reached Nevergreen, but she forgot to get gas and ran out before reaching Lazy Hollow. She told one of her friends about her problems in following the map. He suggested she pay attention to when she could see the mountains, because they are visible only when you are driving north. He also told her that sometimes you can ask the policeman or hitchhiker for directions, and that she should be sure to stop to sleep and eat often enough, because otherwise she is likely to fall asleep at the wheel and drive off the road. Sue was eager to try the Roadtrip game again to see if she could now get to Greenstone.

A SPACESHIP SIMULATION

Simulation programs are used in many science lessons at Babbage School. One such program is a spaceship simulation that introduces seventh- and eighth-grade children to *vectors*. Vectors are forces that have magnitude and direction. They are usually represented by lines. The length of the line represents the force of the vector, and the orientation of the line represents the direction. In the simulation program, students control a spaceship by setting the direction of thrusters and firing them with a specified amount of force. The primary aim of the simulation is to help students develop an intuitive understanding of vectors.

The spaceship program presents various challenges. At the easiest level, the students are to guide a spaceship to a stationary landing platform. To do so, they have to consider the current direction and speed of the spaceship, and determine the angle and strength of the force required to redirect it to the platform. At higher levels, the challenges are more difficult. For example, some levels require the student to land the spaceship on several planets, so different gravitational forces and amounts of atmospheric friction have to be taken into account. The highest level requires docking with another spaceship that is also moving. At each level, students receive points for how quickly and safely they maneuver the spaceship. When students master all the levels, they can play a game in which they fly their spaceship around the solar system in search of treasures.

Bill, a seventh-grade student at Babbage School, recently began using the first level of the spaceship simulation program. When he started the program, the computer displayed a landing platform, a spaceship, and instruments showing the spaceship's direction and speed. To change the direction or speed, Bill pressed the RETURN key. This temporarily stopped the spaceship's motion and suspended time within the simulation. The computer then asked Bill to specify the angle to which the spaceship's thrusters should be turned and the amount of thrust (force) to be applied. To simplify the program, each unit of thrust is equivalent to the force required to move the spaceship at 1 mile per hour. When Bill fired the thrusters, the computer showed the new direction and speed, and the spaceship began moving again.

Bill began by directing the rocket thrusters straight up (i.e., toward 0 degrees) and firing them with a force that set the spaceship into motion at 1,000 miles per hour. The resulting display is shown in Figure 5.5. The landing platform is shown at the upper right of the display; the spaceship is lower and toward the left. The angle and force Bill specified for the thrusters are shown at the lower right; the spaceship's current speed and direction are shown at the left.

When Bill first tried to steer the spaceship to the landing platform, he made a very common error. He waited until the ship was level with the top of the landing platform and then pressed RETURN to direct and fire the thrusters (see Figure 5.6). He set the direction to 90 degrees and fired the thrusters with 1,000 units of thrust. He expected the spaceship to immediately start moving 90 degrees to the right at a speed of 1,000 miles per hour. However, the actual effect is shown in Figure 5.7. The direction of the spaceship was 45 degrees, and the speed was 1,414 miles per hour.

Bill puzzled over what had happened and wondered if he had typed the correct angle. He again set the thrusters to 90 degrees and fired them with 1,000 units of thrust. The result was that the spaceship was directed towards 63 degrees and moving at 2,236 miles per hour.

Once again Bill puzzled over the result, but he suddenly realized what was happening. When the spaceship was going in one direction and he gave it a thrust in another, the resulting direction was between the original one and the angle of the thrust. The speed increased, but not by as much as it would if he fired the thrusters in the exact direction the ship was already going.

Bill thought he now had an idea of how the thrusters controlled the ship. To test his idea, he started the simulation over, set the thrusters to 0 degrees and fired them with 1,000 units of thrust.

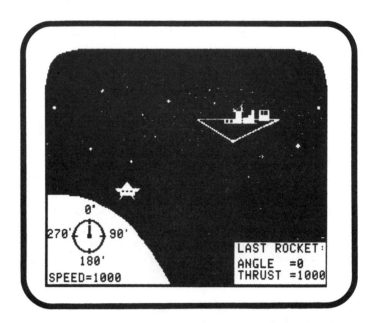

FIGURE 5.5 Starting the spaceship moving up.

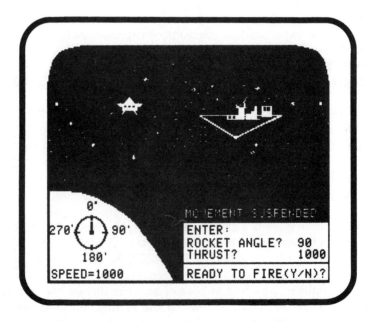

FIGURE 5.6 Firing rocket thrusters, trying to make the spaceship turn 90 degrees.

FIGURE 5.7 The result of combining the 0 degree and 90 degree thrusts.

As he expected, the ship began moving straight up at a speed of 1,000 miles per hour. He then set the thrusters to 180 degrees and fired them, again with 1,000 units of thrust. Sure enough, the spaceship did not go back down, but simply stopped where it was. The downward force and upward force of the same strength had cancelled each other's effects. Bill tried other experiments to confirm his idea and figure out more about controlling the spaceship. He then easily succeeded in guiding the spaceship to the landing platform.

The next day in class, Bill's teacher explained the mathematics of vectors and how they combine. The teacher also showed how to use the mathematical principles to predict exactly how a thrust of a given direction and force will affect the spaceship. After his experience with the spaceship simulation, Bill easily understood his teacher's explanation. Once he learned the mathematical principles, he found the lower levels of the simulation to be too easy, and he advanced to a more difficult level in which he had to land the spaceship on different planets. He began to figure out the interactions of multiple forces, such as the spaceship's motion, the thrusters' force, and a planet's gravitational pull.

ECOLOGY SIMULATIONS

Two simulations are used in studying ecology at Babbage School. In one, students play the role of a National Park Manager. They have a limited budget to deal with problems of wildlife management and erosion while allowing as many people as possible to use the park. Students receive a score that reflects how many people have used the park, how well the ecology has been maintained, and how little money they have spent.

An example of the type of problem the students might have to manage is the erosion of hillsides caused by too many people hiking. The "park manager" can reroute the hiking trails, but that would be expensive. He can choose to restrict the number of people allowed, but limiting people's access to the park reduces the player's score. He can plant shrubs and grass to try to limit the erosion, or close the trails at certain times of the year when erosion is most rapid.

The *National Park Management* program allows the student to try the various options and determine their probable effects before making a final decision. (After all, real park rangers are beginning to use computer simulations to help in these decisions.) The program randomly varies some factors that affect the rate of erosion, such as amount of rain and wind.

Another ecology simulation lets students explore the long-term effects of pollutants on various ecosystems. Students can choose to work with a lake, river, forest or meadow. The computer describes a simplified ecosystem, listing various species, their food supplies, natural enemies and responsiveness to various pollutants. The student can then manipulate the environment by introducing pollutants or other species, or by changing the availability of certain foods. The program asks the student to predict the short-term and long-term results of the changes and then compares the student's prediction with the results predicted by a mathematical model built into the program.

OTHER SIMULATION PROGRAMS

The science classes at Babbage School use several other simulation programs. A chemistry simulation lets students experiment with mixing various types of solutions. An astronomy simulation helps students learn about the constellations and how they look at different times of the year. A flight simulator program enables students to learn how airplanes are controlled (it's a simplified version of a program actually used in training pilots). Another simulation has students build simple machines from components such as gears, levers and pulleys, and then test whether the machines function as planned.

There are also several good history and social studies simulations. One, called *Oregon Trail*, is a simulation of traveling across the United States in the Gold Rush days of the mid-1800s. Students have to select the proper supplies, choose the right trails, plan their trip so they are not caught in the mountains during the winter, carry enough water to get through the desert, deal with dangers posed by animals and nefarious people, and meet other challanges. Still other simulations allow students to experience some aspects of running a business and a political campaign.

CREATING A SIMULATION PROGRAM

Two social studies teachers at Babbage School are developing their own simulation program. They have chosen an ambitious project: simulating a city government. They intend the program to be used by groups of students, each one playing a different role such as mayor, police chief, superintendent of education, city council member, and so on. The entire simulation will cover four years of running a city. The teachers plan to have students use the program for several sessions and then engage in class discussions about city government.

The teachers began designing their program by defining a successfully run city as having a balanced budget; good schools, public transportation and sanitation; and minimal crime. In addition, more people and businesses should be moving to the city than moving away. It seemed complicated to consider all these factors, so the teachers created a mathematical formula that combines them into a single number. This number is used as a score of how well the students run the city. Within the simulation, it is described as the percentage of people who vote for the incumbents in an election at the end of the simulated four years.

The teachers next worked on the aspects of running a city they wanted to include in the simulation. They chose to have the city raise money in four ways: sales taxes, real estate taxes, funds from the state government, and funds from the federal government. The players can allocate the income to departments of education, welfare, police, fire, sanitation, public transit, health, building, and tourism. The student playing the director of each department then decides how to allocate the money within it. The students together comprise a city council, and each student has to convince the city council to allocate sufficient funds to his department.

Since this is to be a realistic simulation, there will not be enough money to keep all city services at an optimal level. The students' task is to make the best overall use of the available funds, not letting one department benefit too much at the expense of others. The teachers are building various types of realistic effects and events into the program. They haven't decided on exactly how many to include, but some of the ones they are thinking about are:

1. The sales tax and real estate tax should have optimal levels. If they are set too low, the city will not have sufficient income. But if they are set too high, city income will also suffer. For example, raising property taxes will cause businesses to leave the city, thereby lowering the tax base.

2. Departments should function more successfully when their employees are highly paid. However, overpaying one group of employees can lead to problems. For example, if the police are given high salaries, the firemen may demand equal pay and go on strike.

3. Certain events will occur on a random basis and the city council will have to reallocate funds. For example, a visit by a foreign dignitary will require many police to work overtime, straining the department's budget. An epidemic will call for extra action by the health department, a gas shortage will cause a crisis in transportation, and so on.

The teachers realize they have a great deal more work in designing the complete simulation, and that actually writing the program in a computer language will be a time consuming and difficult task. However, they believe students will gain a better understanding of the complexities of running a city from this simulation than from books and lectures. They also expect it to be a good catalyst for class discussions, and are eager to hear about the conflicts and problems students encounter, the solutions they propose, and their strategies for governing the simulated city.

Chapter 6

Playful Exercises for the Mind

The teachers at Babbage School believe that the mind, like the body, is strengthened through exercise. They also believe students should enjoy learning, and they encourage students to engage in a wide variety of "playful exercises for the mind." These include creating stories, building models, playing thinking games such as Scrabble and chess, and solving crossword, number, logic and picture puzzles.

Computer programs are used in many of the playful mental activities students enjoy at Babbage School. Various programs provide competitive games, puzzles, fictional worlds for students to explore, and tools that help children create their own puzzles, games, pictures and stories. Each program exercises language, math, memory, visual perception, logical thinking, concentration, creativity, or a combination of these skills.

Computer programs are much more flexible than board games, books or toys. Programs can create different game boards, story events or puzzles each time they are used. They can also vary the complexity of material, the speed with which responses must be made, and the availability of hints and other assistance. Well-designed programs automatically adjust these factors to suit each player, so novices are not frustrated by overly difficult challenges and skilled players are not bored by easy ones. In many games, the computer can take the role of a player and adjust its level of play to provide suitable competition for each individual.

In addition, computers provide powerful tools for students to use in exercising their creativity. Creative tool programs provide frameworks for students to design their own games, create stories and make puzzles for others to solve. These programs are among the most popular ones at Babbage School.

All the mental exercise programs take advantage of the computer's capabilities to capture children's attention and help them learn. Students are intrigued by the fact that they can interact with the computer and their actions determine the computer's response. Many programs hold students' interest with exciting fantasies, as well as attractive graphics, animations, and sounds. Some add computer-synthesized speech. Computers also make games and puzzles more enjoyable by automatically performing chores such as arranging game boards, keeping score, timing responses, enforcing rules, and keeping records when a game is interrupted so it can be restarted at the same point.

In this chapter, I describe a variety of the computerized playful exercises for the mind used at Babbage School. Several related programs that put repetitive drills into game formats are described in Chapter 8.

ADVENTURE GAMES

Adventure games are similar to simulations in that they create, within the computer, a world for people to explore. The key difference is that simulations are based upon real objects and events while adventure games are based upon fictional ones.

Adventure games can be played by an individual or by a group of collaborative players. Players explore the fictional world by commanding a character or alter ego within the game to move and perform certain actions. After each command, the computer presents a description of what the character sees, hears and feels, and where it can move next. Some adventure game programs display pictures of each scene, while others only provide written descriptions.

Each adventure game has main goals, such as finding treasures or reaching certain destinations. Attaining each goal is usually complex, requiring success on a number of subgoals, such as finding maps, keys and other useful objects; avoiding dangers; getting through mazes; and solving various types of problems. The player receives a score that reflects factors such as the amount of the fantasy world he has explored and the number of treasures he has found.

The original adventure games had castles, dungeons, dragons, trolls, wizards and other such entities. The popularity of these adventures led to the development of games set in intergalactic, prehistoric, subterranean, futuristic and other fantasy worlds. Some adventure games have more realistic settings. For example, the player may take the role of a detective searching for clues and questioning witnesses.

Adventure games are one type of *interactive fiction*, a new genre of writing in which the reader plays an active, participatory role, directing or contributing to the story as it unfolds. Other interactive fiction lets readers add their own words, such as the names and descriptions of characters in the story, or select the course the story should follow, such as whether the princess should marry the prince, the pauper or the frog.

Virginia, a sixth-grade child at Babbage School, enjoys an adventure game set in outer space. The scene of the game is a planet on which her character has landed in a damaged spaceship. The object of the game is to find five treasures, repair the spaceship and navigate back to home base. The character within the adventure describes the initial scene:

> I'm in a one-man scoutship. I see a control console and a closed door. There is an exit going down. What shall I do?

Virginia can respond with commands such as: *go down, open door, look around, examine console,* and *take inventory* (to check what items her character is carrying). She types:

EXAMINE CONSOLE

The character responds:

> I see a blue button marked "BLAST OFF" and an unmarked red button.

The interchange then continues (the commands Virginia types are capitalized):

PRESS BLUE BUTTON

> Console replies "Insufficient power." Warning light says "Power crystal damaged."

OPEN DOOR

> I can't open it.

TAKE INVENTORY

Virginia explains she is checking whether there is a key to the door.

I'm carrying nothing at all.

LOOK AROUND

Virginia hopes there is a key hanging on the wall.

I see nothing special.

GO DOWN

I'm in a storage hold. I see a maintenance access hatch, space suit, phaser and shovel. There is an exit going up.

WEAR SUIT

TAKE PHASER

TAKE SHOVEL

Virginia says she figures these will all be useful once she finds her way out of the spaceship.

OPEN HATCH

I can't do that. It's stuck.

SHOOT HATCH

Virginia says maybe shooting it with the phaser will get it unstuck.

I fire the phaser. Nothing happens. Either I missed or beam was absorbed without visible effect.

LOOK AROUND

I see a red button.

PRESS RED BUTTON

The door opens.

ENTER DOOR

I'm in a small airlock. I see a red button by the door, a closed outer door and an open inner door.

PRESS RED BUTTON

There is a "whooshing" sound. The inner door closes and the outer door opens.

GO OUT

I'm outside the airlock on a ledge. The ground is 90 meters below.

Virginia thinks awhile and then says she doesn't see any choice but to jump.

JUMP

I land safely. The gravity here is very weak. I see the scoutship. I can go North, South, East or West.

Virginia says she must remember the gravity is weak, in case she needs to jump up to something later. She also notes that the planet must be very small, since otherwise there would be more gravity.

GO NORTH

I see a cave.

ENTER CAVE

I'm in a large cavern. I see a creature which is about twelve feet tall. It has two legs, wings like a bat and four eyes. Its skin is green and scaly. It makes a horrible shrieking noise. There is an exit going up.

Virginia says that caves are usually interesting in adventure games, so she is going to try to get rid of the creature and explore the cave. Maybe she can destroy it with the phaser.

SHOOT CREATURE

I fire the phaser. Nothing happens. Either I missed or the beam was absorbed without visible effect. The creature is moving toward me. There is an exit going up.

Virginia shoots again with the same result. She then decides to check the phaser, in case something is wrong with it.

EXAMINE PHASER

The phaser has two settings, stun and destroy. It is set on stun.

SET PHASER TO DESTROY

The phaser is now set on destroy.

SHOOT CREATURE

I fire the phaser. The creature falls back with a loud thud. It seems to be unconscious. Behind it there is a strange flickering curtain of light and rock dust.

EXAMINE CURTAIN

It's some sort of force field.

Virginia's next challenge is to find a way through the force field. Perhaps the spacesuit will protect her or maybe she can deflect the force field with the shovel. Once she gets past the force field, there are many caverns to explore and treasures to find. One of the treasures is a crystal that can replace the damaged power crystal on the spaceship. She will then have to return to the ship and figure out how to put the new crystal into place.

Adventure worlds can be complex, with a wide variety of scenes, objects and characters. Playing an adventure game is similar to reading a science fiction or fantasy story, but the reader actively influences the story by exploring the fantasy world and interacting with its characters and objects.

Adventure games encourage children to read and actively think about what they read. The information obtained helps them advance in the game, so children try to understand and remember it. Players also learn to pay close attention to details, since there is often information that becomes important later in the game. For example, in the game Virginia was playing, she found some crystals in the cave. Only by remembering that the spaceship's power crystal was damaged could she realize the need to take the crystals back to the ship.

In addition to encouraging reading, adventure games provide a suitable format for many types of learning. They may require the player to solve particular types of logical problems or use specific knowledge. For example, Virginia might need to know about the solar system in order to navigate back to home base.

One adventure game used at Babbage School was designed specifically for education. It contains a wizard who appears at certain places and asks questions. If the player answers the questions correctly, he will receive a useful hint. If he answers incorrectly, he may lose a treasure or have an evil spell cast upon him. The teachers can enter their own questions for the wizard to ask. They also specify the answers the wizard is to accept, how many chances to give the player, and how severe a penalty to impose for incorrect answers.

FACEMAKER

Facemaker is a program for young children that combines a creative tool with a memory game. The child begins by creating a face. The program presents sets of facial features—mouths, noses, ears, eyes and hair. The child selects features and the computer combines them into a face. Figure 6.1 shows a partially completed face, with the selection of eyes available for the child to choose. Children enjoy making funny faces and faces that look like people they know.

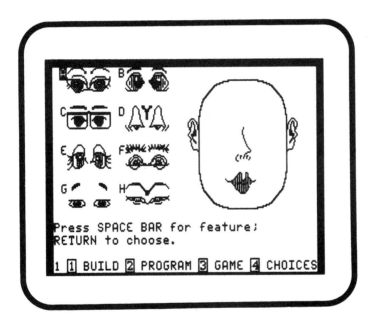

FIGURE 6.1   *Facemaker* program. The child can select any of the eyes shown.

Once a face is made, the child can make it move. Facemaker provides a very simple computer language with the following commands:

S = smile E = ear wiggle
F = frown C = cry
W = wink $-$ = delay
T = stick tongue out

The child writes an animation program by typing a sequence of these letters, using the dash to make the face pause between actions. For example, the child might type:

SWFS

to make the face smile, wink, frown, and then smile again.

The Facemaker program also incorporates a memory game analogous to the game called *Simon*. In this game, the computer shows the face performing a sequence of actions. The child tries to remember the actions and type the letters that correspond to them. For example, if the face winks and smiles, the child should type WS. Each time the child is correct, one more action is added to the sequence. That is, after the child types WS, the computer might make the face wink, smile and cry. The child should then type WSC. The sequence of actions continues to become longer until the child does not type the correct letters. The aim of the game is for the child to reproduce as long a sequence as he can.

PINBALL CONSTRUCTION SET™

A very popular program at Babbage School lets children design and create their own computerized pinball games. Once they have created a game, they can play it, using a joystick to shoot the ball into play and work the flippers.

A student named Max demonstrated that when the program begins three types of elements appear on the computer screen. At the left is a box in the basic shape of a pinball game. At the right are pictures of the available tools, such as a hand, hammer, scissors and paint brush. In between are the pieces for the pinball game—flippers, bumpers, launchers, barricades, spinners, targets and others. Max used the tools and pieces to construct a game, test-playing it as he went along. Figure 6.2 shows the computer screen as Max worked on his game.

Max began constructing his game by using the joystick to control the hand on the screen. He could move the hand to a pinball piece, press the joystick button to pick up the piece, move it anywhere on the game board, and press the button again to release the piece. In Figure 6.2, the hand is shown in the middle of the board, having just placed a round bumper.

Max used the arrow, scissors and hammer to change the shape of the game board and the barricades. He used the paint brush to color the pieces and board. He placed three targets where they would be difficult to hit and then used special tools to link them together and set bonus points. He explained that he made it so if you hit all three targets you get 10,000 bonus points.

Max also used a special feature of the pinball program that let him experiment with changing the physics of the world in which the game is played. He could, for example, set gravity to be high or low. When gravity was low, the ball looked very light, almost as if it were floating. When gravity was high, the ball moved as if it were very heavy, dropping quickly to the bottom of the board. Max also could change the time (putting the game into fast or slow motion), the bounce of the ball, and the elasticity of the bumpers. He experimented with changing gravity, bounce and elasticity, and he explored how these three factors interact.

Max spent a long time working on his pinball game. He was eager to create a game his friends would find fun and challenging, but realized this would not be an easy task. He carefully considered the shape of the playing area and barricades, and the number and

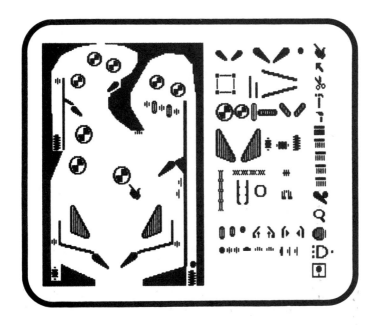

FIGURE 6.2   Pinball Construction Set Program.

locations of flippers, bumpers, targets and other pinball parts he selected. He made sure the point value assigned to each reflected how easy or difficult it was to hit. He checked that the ball in his game had a good amount of bounce, that players had ample opportunities to use their flippers, that there was an appropriate risk of losing the ball, and that the sound effects and colors were varied and interesting. He tested the program, finding and changing several places where the ball could get stuck or be caught in an endlessly repeating pattern of bounces. While creating his game, Max did a great deal of thinking, experimenting, testing, problem solving and revising. He was very pleased when his friends said it was the best game any of them had made so far.

LANGUAGE EXPLORER

Language Explorer is a program used in teaching beginning reading and foreign languages. This program lets children learn about words through exploration and play, and then use the words to create animated stories.

The program contains sets of words, divided into nouns, verbs, adjectives and adverbs. There is a picture corresponding to each noun and an action corresponding to each verb. When the child types a noun, a picture of the corresponding object appears on the screen. When the child types a noun and a verb, an animated picture shows the object performing the action specified by the verb. Features of the objects, such as their size and color, and aspects of the actions, such as their speed and direction, can be changed by adding adjectives and adverbs.

The teacher selects one of the sets of words built into the program and has the computer print a list of the words for the child. The words in the list are grouped according to syntactic category, but the child is not given labels such as nouns or verbs. His task is to discover the effects of each word on the picture and figure out how the words in each category are similar.

Eight-year-old Chang's native language is Chinese. He has been at Babbage School for four months and has already mastered a great deal of English. He enjoys the Language Explorer program and finds it helps him learn quickly. Table 6.1 shows a word list Chang has been exploring recently.

Since Chang has worked with this program before, he knew that the first set of words in the list would be names of things and that a picture would appear when he typed one of these

TABLE 6.1
Sample Word List from Language Explorer Program

BOY
GIRL
MONKEY
HORSE
PIG
COW
GIRAFFE
BEAR
SQUIRREL
BIRD

WALK
RUN
FLY
JUMP
FALL

BIG
SMALL
TINY

QUICKLY
SLOWLY
UP
DOWN
LEFT
RIGHT

words. He went through the list of nouns, carefully typing the letters to spell each one correctly, and studied the pictures that appeared. He pronounced most of the words correctly, but asked his teacher for assistance with *squirrel* and *giraffe*. After typing all the nouns, he began combining nouns and verbs, laughing at many of the pictures such as the boy flying, the monkey falling and the bird jumping. He thought watching the animals fall and fly was particularly funny, and systematically combined each of the nouns with those two verbs.

He then began to explore the effects of the adjectives and adverbs. He first typed the words:

BOY WALK BIG QUICKLY

The computer responded by displaying:

***** BOY WALK *****

From his prior experience with this program, Chang understood that this meant he had typed the words in the wrong order. He then tried:

QUICKLY BOY WALK BIG

The computer again showed:

***** BOY WALK *****

Finally Chang tried:

BIG BOY WALK QUICKLY

and was pleased to see the animated picture on the screen. He tried some of the other adjectives and adverbs. He particularly enjoyed using *tiny* and *quickly* and watching the "baby" animals scurry across the screen.

The teacher explained that at the level Chang was working, the program requires the words in the correct order but does not require all the details of correct sentence syntax. At the next level, Chang would have to type:

THE BIG BOY WALKS QUICKLY

before the computer would show the picture. The teacher also explained that there are many other sets of words available in the program. For example, one set introduces the distinction between *animate* nouns, such as *boy*, *dog* and *horse*, and *inanimate* nouns, such as *table*, *house* and *ball*. Another set introduces *transitive* verbs, so the child can form sentences such as "The boy pushed the horse."

Once Chang mastered his set of words, he created an animated story with the following sequence:

TINY BIRD WALK

SQUIRREL WALK

TINY BIRD FLY QUICKLY

MONKEY WALK

SQUIRREL RUN QUICKLY

BIG BEAR

MONKEY RUN QUICKLY

BOY WALK

BEAR RUN QUICKLY

Chang spent some time entering all the words and correcting his typing and spelling errors. He then typed the word STORY to make the computer display the pictures. The computer showed one picture at a time, waiting for Chang to press the RETURN key before going on to the next one. Chang narrated an elaborated version of the story, saying that the squirrel scared the tiny bird, but was then scared by the monkey. The bear scared the monkey, and then the boy scared the bear.

SECRET CODES PROGRAM

A language program called *Secret Codes* is a favorite mental exercise of some children at Babbage School. When using this program, students work with sets of rules for changing messages into secret codes. This helps them learn about letter and word patterns, about sequences of rules such as those used in linguistics and computer science, and about developing and testing hypotheses while solving problems.

The program has two main options, *Code Breaker* and *Code Maker*. When the *Code Breaker* option is selected, players try to figure out the rules to an existing code. The code can be one created by another person or one created by the computer. When the *Code Maker* option is selected, players make their own codes, using a special computer language designed for this purpose. Children play games creating codes for each other to try to break. Some groups have developed elaborate coding schemes so they can exchange secret messages.

Leroy, an eighth-grader at Babbage School, recently tried the Secret Codes program. To begin, he selected the Code Breaker option and had the computer create a simple code. Leroy typed messages in English, and the computer responded with the coded versions. His aim was to select messages that let him figure out the rules to the code. When he thought he knew the rules, he would press a special key. The computer would then test whether he knew the rules by giving him English sentences to translate into code and coded sentences to translate into English.

Leroy began by typing:

THIS IS A TEST.

The computer responded with the coded version of this sentence:

ESTA A SI HISTA.

Leroy first wondered whether one of the rules of the code changes IS to A and A to SI. To test this hypthesis, he typed:

A IS

The computer responded with:

SI A

so Leroy figured he was correct. He then typed:

TESTING ONE TWO THREE FOUR.
and the computer replied:

OURFA HREETA WOTA NEO ESTINGTA.

Leroy puzzled over how TESTING was converted to OURFA. He suddenly realized the OURFA has the same letters as FOUR, plus an additional A. He checked and found the next two words of the coded messages to have the same letters as THREE and TWO, respectively, except that each had an additional A. Examining them more carefully, he figured out that the code moves the first letter to the end of the word and then adds an A. He also realized that the code reverses the order of the words; TESTING ONE TWO THREE FOUR became FOUR THREE TWO ONE TESTING.

At this point, Leroy thought the code had three rules:

1. Reverse the order of the words in the sentence.

2. For each word, move the first letter to the end.

3. Add A to each word.

He then checked carefully and found that these rules did not work for some of the words: ONE became NEO, IS became SI and A did not change at all. He noticed that all these words did not have an A added to them and that they were all three letters or shorter. He figured he had to change his third rule to:

3. If the word has more than three letters, then add an A.

Leroy was sure he now had the right rules, so he pressed the ESCAPE key to signal the computer that he was ready for a test. The computer typed:

CHANGE THIS SENTENCE INTO THE CODE:
SUE RAN TO SCHOOL BUT SHE FORGOT ONE OF HER BOOKS.

Leroy took a few minutes to work out how his three rules would change this sentence. His first rule was to reverse the order of the words, so he wrote out:

BOOKS HER OF ONE FORGOT SHE BUT SCHOOL TO RAN SUE.

The second rule was to move the first letter of each word to the end, so he wrote:

OOKSB ERH FO NEO ORGOTF HES UTB CHOOLS OT ANR UES.

The third rule was to add A to each word that has more than three letters. Leroy applied this rule and got:

OOKSBA ERH FO NEO ORGOTFA HES UTB CHOOLSA OT ANR UES.

Leroy typed his coded sentence into the computer. He was surprised when the computer replied:

I'M SORRY, BUT YOU HAVE NOT FIGURED OUT THE CODE.
YOU CODED 5 OF THE 11 WORDS CORRECTLY.

Leroy returned to trying to break the code by typing English sentences for the computer to transform. He was eager to see what the code would be for the test sentence and so he typed:

SUE RAN TO SCHOOL BUT SHE FORGOT ONE OF HER BOOKS.

The computer responded with the correct coded version:

OOKSBA ERHA FO NEO ORGOTHA HESA UTBA CHOOLSA OTA ANRA UESA.

After further thought and several more test sentences, Leroy found the error in his rules. The third one should have been:

3. If the word ends in a consonant, then add an A.

With this new rule, Leroy was able to correctly convert all the test sentences. He then started to figure out how to create his own code, so he could exchange secret messages with his friends.

PUZZLE AND GAME PROGRAMS

Children enjoy puzzles and games, and many teachers use these activities to help motivate and teach their students. At Babbage School, computer programs are used to create puzzles and games that involve picture recognition, language, math, logic and problem solving skills. Descriptions of some of the most popular ones follow.

What Is It?

A program called *What Is It?* requires skill at recognizing pictures of objects from minimal visual cues. The program comes with many sets of pictures, such as animals, plants, furniture and state maps. Students and teachers can add their own pictures to the program, using graphics creation tools such as those described in Chapter 3.

The computer begins by displaying a small percentage of the dots that make up the picture, and it gradually adds more. An example picture is shown in Figure 6.3. The players can set the speed at which dots are added. Students compete, seeing who can recognize each picture first. A player receives points for each correct answer, and the faster he answers the more points he receives. If a player enters an incorrect answer, the computer deducts points from his score.

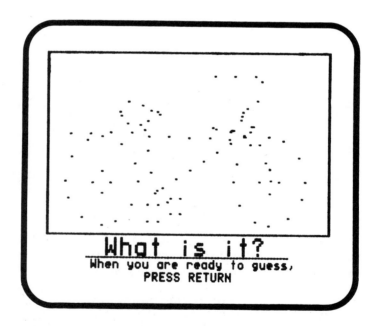

FIGURE 6.3 An example from the *What Is It?* program. The object shown is a bicycle.

Language Puzzles

Programs are available at Babbage School for creating crossword, anagram and word search puzzles. Each program lets the teacher or student enter a list of words. It then arranges the words into one or more puzzles. Teachers use these programs with current vocabulary and spelling lists. Children like to make their own puzzles with names of friends, sports heroes, or other words.

Figure 6.4 shows a crossword puzzle on the computer screen. A student enters the words and the computer arranges them into the puzzle format. Then it goes through the words one-by-one and has the student enter the clues. In Figure 6.4, the student has just entered the clue for the word *printer*. When all the clues are entered, the computer will print a puzzle page and an answer key page.

Figure 6.5 shows another language program called *Raise the Flags*. This is a variation of the game called *Hangman*. The student's challenge is to figure out the word the computer has selected. The student can guess one letter at a time. If the letter is in the word, the character shown on the computer screen will raise a flag

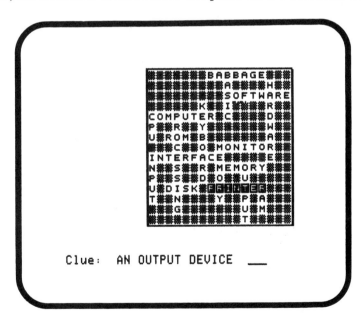

FIGURE 6.4 Making a crossword puzzle. The clue for *printer* has just been entered.

FIGURE 6.5   *Raise the Flags* program.

showing where the letter appears. The object of the game is to get all the correct flags raised with as few guesses as possible. As with the other programs, the students and teachers can enter their own word lists.

Darts

Darts is a math game that gives children practice working with fractions. The computer displays a vertical number line, with 0 marked at the bottom and 1 at the top. Along the line, there are pictures of three balloons. The child types a fraction, and a dart moves to that point on the number line. The goal of the game is to pop all the balloons with the fewest darts possible.

Figure 6.6 shows an example of the display screen. The child has already entered three fractions: 7/8, 2/5 and 3/16, but has not hit any balloons. The computer is waiting for the child to enter a fraction to direct his next dart.

Coordinate Monsters

The *Coordinate Monsters* game is used in several math classes at Babbage School. The computer presents a coordinate grid with monsters pictured on it (see Figure 6.7). The child controls a "mon-

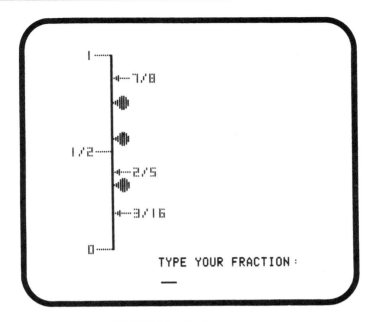

FIGURE 6.6   Darts program.

ster-masher," which he directs to move to the locations of monsters on the grid.

There are three levels to the game. At the simplest level, the child types the X,Y (horizontal, vertical) coordinates of each monster. The monster-masher moves to those coordinates and removes a monster if one is present. For example, in the display in Figure 6.7 the child could enter the coordinates $-3, -4$ (three steps left of center and four steps down from center) and remove the snake-like monster at the lower left.

At the second level, the child must direct the masher to move from its current position to each monster. For example, if the masher is at location $-3, -4$ and the child wants to remove the other snake-like monster which is at coordinates 2,2, he would have to enter 5,6. This would tell the masher to move 5 steps to the right and 6 steps up.

At the highest level, the child enters a formula and the masher moves along the line plotted by that formula. For example, if the child enters $Y = X/2$, the monster would move along the line shown in Figure 6.8, removing any monsters it passes over. The child's aim is to remove all the monsters while using as few formulas as possible. This game leads some children to work with complex formulas. Figure 6.9 shows an example.

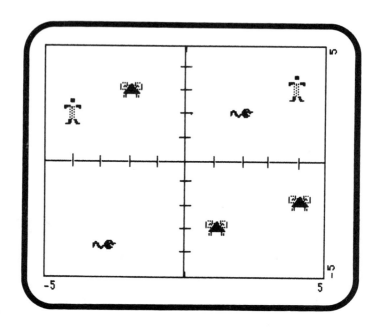

FIGURE 6.7 *Coordinate Monsters* board.

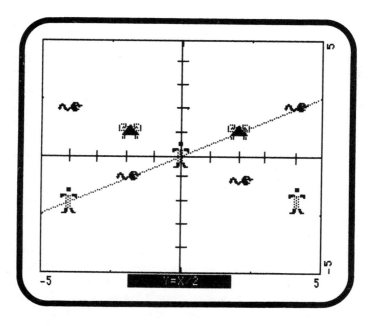

FIGURE 6.8 A simple formula for the *Monster Masher*.

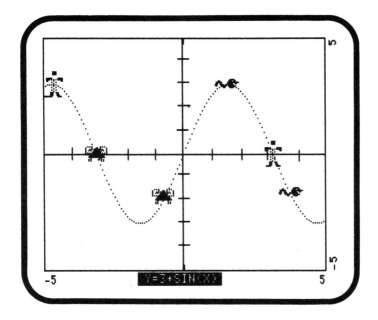

FIGURE 6.9 A more complex formula for the *Monster Masher.*

Maxit

Some of the students enjoy a game called *Maxit*, which requires math skills and strategic thinking. The computer presents a grid of numbers and a marker, as shown in Figure 6.10. Players alternate selecting numbers from the board. As each number is selected, it is removed from the board and added to the player's score. The player with the highest score at the end of the game wins.

The first player can move the marker horizontally to select any number in the row. This player cannot move vertically, so he is limited to choosing one of the numbers in the row in which the marker is located at the start of his turn. The second player can only move vertically, so he must choose a number in the column in which the marker is located at the start of his turn. As in chess or checkers, to play the game well players have to look ahead as many turns as possible: "If I take the 5 in this row, you will probably take the 5 in that column, but then I could take the 8...." The children can also select to play with a time limit for each move.

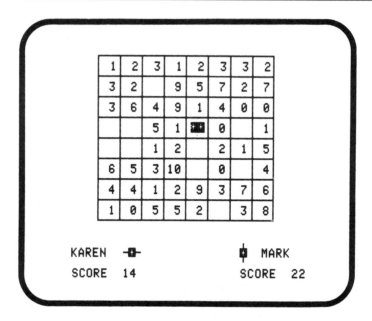

FIGURE 6.10 *Maxit* game board.

The computer will then serve as the timer and automatically deduct points from players' scores if they go over the limit.

Each time the game is played, the students select the range of numbers to be used and the computer randomly arranges the board. If one child wants to play and cannot find a partner, the computer can take the role of a player. The child chooses any of five levels for the computer's play. At level 1, the computer simply takes the highest available number, without regard for what will happen on the next move. At level 2, the computer checks one move ahead to see what numbers the player will be able to take. At level 3, it checks two moves ahead. At levels 4 and 5 the computer uses more complex strategies. After some practice, most of the children are able to beat the computer at levels 1 and 2 and some can win at level 3. They rarely win against the computer at levels 4 and 5. Some students have spent a lot of time trying to figure out the strategies the computer is programmed to follow at the highest two levels.

What's Next?

The *What's Next?* program presents logical problems for students to solve. Each problem contains pictures of characters with

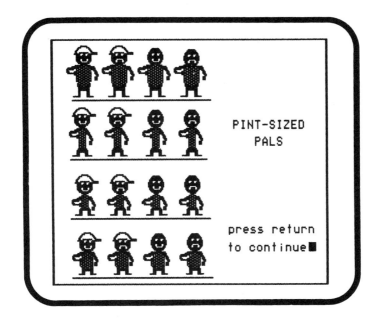

FIGURE 6.11 The set of characters for the *What's Next?* program.

different attributes. One set is shown in Figure 6.11. In this example set, half of the characters are fat and half are thin; half are tall and half are short; half are smiling and half are frowning; and half have hats and half are hatless. The computer presents sequences of these characters. Their order within the sequence is determined by certain rules. Students try to figure out the rules and tell the computer which character comes next.

Figure 6.12 shows a simple example. The computer has presented a sequence of five characters. All are fat, tall and hatless. They alternate whether they are smiling or frowning, and the last one is smiling. Therefore, the next character should be fat, tall, hatless and frowning.

Figure 6.13 shows a slightly more complex example in which two attributes change. All the characters are fat and smiling. The first two are hatless, the second two have hats, and the third two are hatless. Therefore, the next one is probably going to have a hat. The characters alternate between short and tall. The last one is short, so the next one should be tall. The child should enter that the next character is fat, smiling, tall and wearing a hat. This program

FIGURE 6.12   A *What's Next?* problem in which one attribute changes.

FIGURE 6.13   A *What's Next?*   problem in which two attributes change.

can also present more complex problems in which the characters are arranged into rows and columns.

Square Pairs

Square Pairs is a memory and concentration game. The program displays a board with numbered boxes, each containing a word, number or picture. The contents of each box matches the contents of another box on the board. On each turn, a player selects two boxes, trying to find those with matching pairs. To play the game well, players must remember where each item is located and recognize when items match. Sometimes the game is played with exact matches so, for example, the word *dog* might appear in two boxes. More often, it is played with matching pairs, so, for example, the word *dog* might be paired with its Spanish translation, *perro*.

The teachers and students can put their own words, numbers and pictures into the game, and choose how many matching pairs are included. Therefore, this program can be used in many classes and by children of all ages. The youngest children play the game matching upper-case to lower-case letters, or simple words to pictures. In French class it is played with translations from English

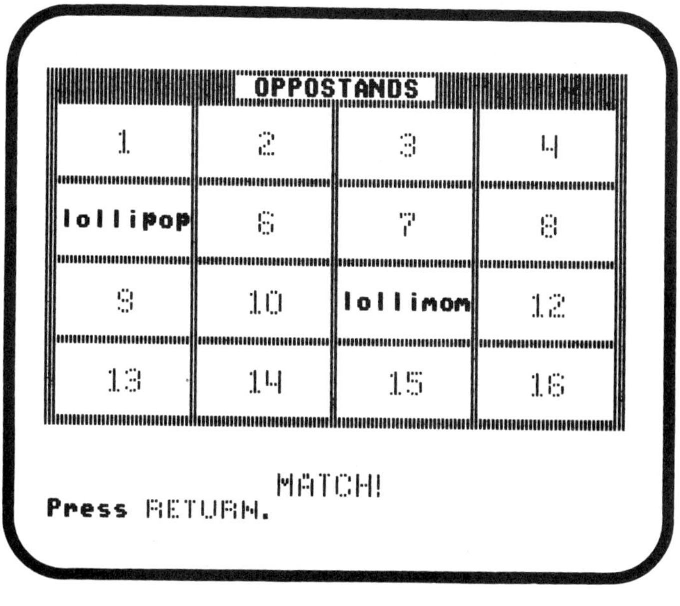

FIGURE 6.14 *Square Pairs* game board.

to French or with French synonyms or antonyms. In math class it is played with math problems in some boxes and matching answers in others. In geography class it is played with country and capital city matches; in history class it is played with matching events and people. Some of the children have created puzzle games with matches such as words and anagrams. Other games have been created with funny word matches (see Figure 6.14).

Each time the game is played, the computer randomly arranges the board, keeps track of which matches have been found, and keeps score. The program also allows the computer to take the role of one player. When serving as a player, the computer adjusts its level of play to give different children appropriate levels of competition.

CONCLUSION

Programs that enable children to play adventure games; create with tools such as Facemaker and the Pinball Construction Set; explore words and work with secret codes; make puzzles; and play math, language, logic and memory games, provide a wide variety of playful mental exercises. Each program takes advantage of the flexible and interactive nature of computers. Students enjoy and actively participate in these playful exercises, and while doing so they develop their mental abilities.

Chapter 7

Computerized Lessons

Teachers, books, films and computers can all present material for students to learn. Each of these means of presenting lessons has its own advantages and disadvantages. Which one is best on any particular occasion depends upon the nature of the material to be learned; the preferred learning styles of the students; and the quality of the available teachers, books, films, and computer programs.

Teachers have the potential to motivate students, stimulate their curiosity, and bolster their confidence. Teachers can encourage students to learn, direct their attention to suitable areas of study, reward their efforts, and when necessary cajole or compel them to study. These roles of teachers will never be fulfilled by computers. Students will always prefer smiles and compliments from an admired teacher to smile faces and positive messages displayed on a computer screen.

Teachers can be much more flexible and responsive than books, films or computers. Since they know their students and can interact with them, teachers are best able to tailor lessons to fit the individuals in their classes. Skilled teachers make sure students have the background knowledge required to understand each lesson, and they adapt their presentations to an appropriate level and pace. They direct students to focus upon the important parts of lessons, and they use examples and analogies that are familiar to their students. During a lesson, teachers observe and interact with students, asking them questions and noting when they look puzzled or inattentive. Teachers are then able to alter the lesson while they present it, repeating, clarifying and elaborating as necessary.

Unfortunately, in most cases teachers have to address many students at a time and so cannot fully tailor their lessons to each individual. Furthermore, the opportunity for teachers and students to interact results in potential difficulties as well as advantages. There will always be teachers and students who have conflicts with each other, and when this is the case the student's interest in school and learning may be discouraged.

Books have advantages and disadvantages that are very different from those of teachers. Books can make the knowledge of experts available to everyone. They also give readers complete control to choose when and how they read. Each reader can proceed at his own rate, reading important information carefully, rereading when necessary, and skimming over less critical material. However, these advantages are tied to certain disadvantages. Each book is addressed to a varied audience, not tailored to individual readers. Books also lack any interactiveness; they cannot respond to readers' thoughts, questions and actions. Another practical disadvantage of books is that many students are not proficient at learning by reading, and therefore cannot make good use of the information in books.

Films and television programs have the advantages of powerful visual and auditory presentations that hold students' interest. Films can bring sights and sounds from anywhere to the viewer, and they can convey information in interesting and easily understood ways. However, films, like books, must be designed for a typical viewer and do not respond or adapt to individuals.

ADVANTAGES OF COMPUTERS

Computers can be programmed to have many of the advantages and avoid many of the disadvantages of teachers, books and films. Well-designed programs give computers some of the flexibility and responsiveness that is available from teachers but lacking with books and films. Computers can evaluate students' knowledge before beginning a lesson and closely monitor their learning as the lesson progresses. Computers can adapt the level of the material, the speed of presentation, and the amount of repetition to be appropriate for each individual. Computers, like books, can allow each student to work at his own pace, and they can make experts' knowledge of a subject available to everyone. Computers can also use pictures, animations and sound. Although the pictures and sounds are rudimentary when compared to those of films, they can help convey new concepts and hold students' interest. Recently, computers have been combined with video disks, making it possible to coordinate movie-quality pictures and sounds with computerized lessons.

Computers also have the advantage of being completely objective, feeling no frustration or impatience with difficult students. This, combined with the interacting, individualizing, and attention-holding capabilities, makes computers especially valuable teaching tools for students who have learning problems.

Computerized lessons are available in many subject areas at Babbage School. These lessons are used in several different ways. Sometimes they are the principal means of teaching a particular topic. More often, they supplement other lessons, are used for review, or are an option for the children who prefer them. Some teachers also use computers with large display screens as visual aids while they present lessons. For example, one math teacher uses a computer to display graphs of equations. She finds this to be quicker and more accurate than drawing the graphs on a chalk board or transparencies.

AN EXAMPLE LESSON

Carolyn, a seventh-grader at Babbage School, prefers computerized lessons to books or teachers' presentations. She has trouble keeping her attention on books and often feels that teachers present material too quickly. She is embarrassed to interrupt and ask teachers to repeat what they have said. With the computer, she can work at her own pace and have things repeated as many times as she needs. Carolyn may take a little longer for each lesson than other students, but with the computer this doesn't matter, and she learns the material well.

In science class, Carolyn has been working with computerized biology lessons. The biology lesson program is a comprehensive one that presents lessons, asks questions to check whether the student understands the material, and keeps track of each student's progress. Carolyn has completed eleven lessons in which she learned about the skeletal, muscular, nervous, respiratory, and digestive systems. She has just completed the first section on the circulation system and is about to begin studying the heart and blood vessels.

The program displays a small amount of information on the screen at a time, waits for Carolyn to respond, and then adds more information. As each interchange is finished, the computer clears the screen so there is no extra information to distract her. This helps Carolyn focus her attention on the right part of the lesson, something she has trouble doing when reading a book. The program lets Carolyn work at her own pace and it provides assistance when she needs it. When the computer asks a question that Carolyn cannot answer, she types HELP. The computer then repeats the relevant part of a lesson, provides a hint or gives the answer.

When Carolyn uses the program, it begins by asking her to type her name and her teacher's name. The computer then looks up her record (which is automatically saved on a disk as she does each lesson) to determine where to start. Last time she used this program, Carolyn had completed the lesson about the blood. Therefore, the program begins by checking whether she recalls the material well enough to proceed to the next lesson. It will not let her go on to the next lesson until she passes a quiz on the previous one.

The program begins with:

Hello Carolyn. Last time you finished the lesson on the blood. Are you ready for a quiz, or would you like a review first?
Type Q for a quiz or R for a review.

Carolyn thinks she remembers the lesson well, so she selects the quiz. The program then displays a series of questions. After each question, it waits for Carolyn's answer and it then provides feedback. Carolyn's interaction with the computer is shown below (her responses are italicized).

Quiz on the Blood:
Question #1. What are the four main components of blood?

Red cells, white cells, plasma and platelets

Very good Carolyn. You named all four correctly.
***

(*** in the text marks when the computer waits for Carolyn to press the RETURN key. It then clears the screen and displays the next question or statement.)

Question #2. Which component works to close breaks in blood vessels?

White blood cells

No Carolyn, that's not the function of the white blood cells. Please try again.

Platelets

That's right. Good.
***

Question #3. What do the white blood cells do?

Fight disease and infection

That's right. The white blood cells help defend the body against micro-organisms.
***

Question #4. Which component of the blood carries oxygen to the body cells?

Red blood cells

That's true, but which of the four main components of red blood cells carries oxygen?

Hemoglobin

That's right.
***

Question #5. Which component of the blood carries nutrients and vitamins to the body cells?

Plasma

Very good Carolyn.
That's the end of the quiz. You did very well.
***

Now you are ready to study how blood moves around the body. Would you like to start this lesson now?

Yes

At the beginning of the lesson, the computer presents some basic information and asks questions to check whether Carolyn understands how the circulatory system connects to the systems she has already studied. As in the quiz, a small amount of information is displayed on the screen at a time, the computer waits for Carolyn to finish and press the RETURN key, and then it clears the screen and presents the next piece of the lesson. This procedure allows Carolyn to work at her own pace, and it helps her focus her attention on each element of the lesson.

Biology Lesson #12: The Circulatory System

The circulatory system moves blood around the body. It carries the blood to all the muscles and organs of the

body. The blood brings oxygen and nutrients to the cells, and it takes waste products away from them.
***
The circulatory system works with other systems of the body. Do you remember which system provides oxygen for the blood?

Respiration

That's right Carolyn. The respiratory system brings oxygen into the body.
***
Do you know what system provides nutrients for the blood?

Digestive

Very good. The digestive system brings nutrients into the body.
***
The parts of the circulatory system covered in this lesson are the heart and the blood vessels. The two main types of blood vessels are veins and arteries.
***
What is the function of the heart?

Pumps blood

Good. The heart is a pump.
***
What is the function of the veins?

Carries blood

Yes, but do the veins carry blood toward the heart or away from the heart?

Help

The veins carry blood to the heart. Arteries carry blood away from the heart.
***

Next, the program uses graphics and animation. The following screen displays show some of the lesson materials and questions, and Carolyn's responses.

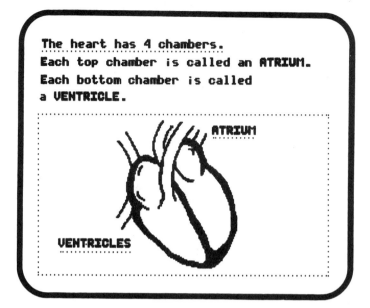

FIGURE 7.1

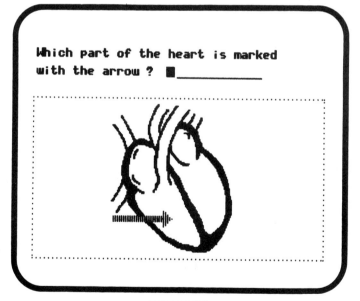

FIGURE 7.2

Carolyn responds *Ventricle.*

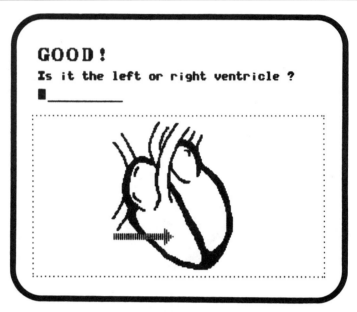

FIGURE 7.3

Carolyn responds *Left ventricle*, which is incorrect. The computer then presents a display to show Carolyn which side is left and which side is right in the figure.

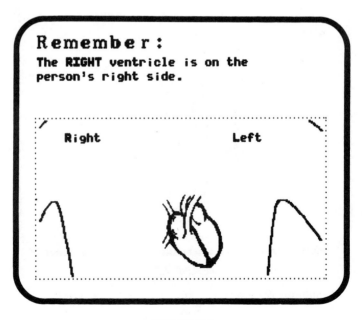

FIGURE 7.4

It then returns to the previous question, and Carolyn enters the correct answer. The lesson continues:

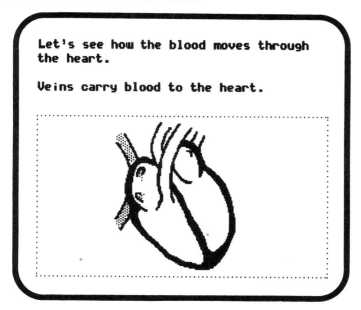

FIGURE 7.5

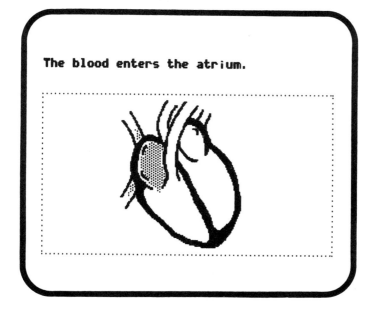

FIGURE 7.6

The blood flows into the ventricle.

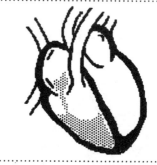

FIGURE 7.7

The valve between the atrium and the
ventricle closes.
The muscles of the ventricle contract,
sending blood to the lungs.

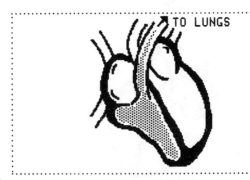

TO LUNGS

FIGURE 7.8

Next, the program illustrates and explains the two circuits of blood vessels in the body. Carolyn learns that the *pulmonary circuit* carries blood between the heart and the lungs, and the *systemic circuit* carries blood between the heart and all the other parts of the body. The description of the flow of blood through the body is accompanied by pictures and animations. In the animations, the computer displays the name of each major organ and blood vessel as the blood cells enter them. Oxygenated blood is shown in red and deoxygenated blood in blue.

After the program introduces and illustrates all the main parts of the system, it reviews and tests Carolyn's knowledge. It displays an animation of a blood cell moving through the body. At certain points, the animation stops and Carolyn is asked to type the name of the location of the blood cell.

In the final part of the lesson, Carolyn controls the operation of the circulation system displayed on the computer screen. It's almost like a video game. Carolyn uses a joystick to direct the movement of a blood cell and she presses certain keys to open or close the valves; contract or expand the ventrical muscles; or have the blood and body cells exchange oxygen, carbon dioxide, nutrients and waste products. The program asks Carolyn to trace various paths, such as how a blood cell could travel from the left lung, through the heart, to the stomach. Carolyn makes several mistakes when she begins, such as forgetting to press the keys that signal that the ventricle muscles should contract or that the blood should get oxygen at the lungs. At each mistake, the program stops the animation, points out the error, and moves the blood cell back so Carolyn can make the system work correctly.

This segment of a biology lesson shows some of the capabilities of computers to present lessons. A good computerized lesson creates a dialogue between the student and the computer. The computer monitors the student's learning and adjusts the lesson accordingly. When the student is unable to answer a question, the computer provides hints, elaborations and clarifications. The computer can also be programmed to use graphics and animations, and to let the student control the display, as when Carolyn directed the actions of the circulatory system.

CREATING COMPUTERIZED LESSONS WITH AUTHORING SYSTEMS

Before a computer can present a lesson, someone must create a program that tells the computer exactly what to do at every point in the lesson. The program controls the text, pictures and sounds presented by the computer. It determines which questions the computer asks and when it asks them. A good program recognizes all answers, both correct and incorrect, students are likely to give. It also checks for common errors and provides appropriate hints, repetitions and clarifications. This can be difficult, since students often produce unexpected answers or unique spellings of correct answers, and each student is subject to his own misinformation and misinterpretations. The program also tells the computer when to have students proceed to the next part of the lesson and whether it should store information about the students' progress.

Creating a program for a lesson as complex as Carolyn's biology one is a difficult task that requires a team of curriculum developers, software designers and programmers. However, individual teachers can create their own smaller scale lessons.

Computerized lessons can be created with any programming language. One language, called PILOT, is designed especially for this purpose. However, using a programming language to create lessons is too time-consuming and tedious for most teachers. Fortunately, certain types of lessons can be created quickly and easily without programming, through the use of *lesson authoring systems*.

Authoring systems take advantage of the fact that most lessons follow a similar format: Information is presented, questions are asked, the student answers and receives feedback, and then the cycle is repeated. Authoring systems are sophisticated programs that provide frameworks into which teachers can enter their own lesson materials. That is, the structure of the lesson has already been programmed and the teachers simply add the content. While it is easier to create a lesson with an authoring system than with a programming language, the nature of the lesson is constrained by the formats built into the authoring system.

Authoring systems vary in their flexibility and their ease of use. Many provide the capability for multiple choice, true/false and fill-in questions, as well as math problems. Often, these systems allow teachers to include hints, second chances, and branches to different parts of the lesson. Some provide the capability to add pictures, animations and sounds. Authoring systems may also automatically keep records of how many questions each student answers correctly.

Several teachers at Babbage School use a lesson authoring system to create computerized lessons on specific topics. The authoring system prompts the teacher for what information to enter when, and it automatically forms the information into a lesson. Some of the older students also use the authoring systems to create lessons for their classmates and for the younger children.

Mr. Stevenson, a sixth-grade teacher at Babbage School, often uses lesson authoring systems. In one case, he created a geography lesson for his students. The authoring system he used is a simple one. It works with written presentations only, and does not allow pictures or sounds.

When Mr. Stevenson begins creating his lesson, the computer first prompts him to enter the text which would introduce the first questions:

Enter text for first set of questions:

Mr. Stevenson responds:

This lesson is about U.S. geography. First, I'm going to ask you some questions to find out how much you already know.

Then the dialog continues with the computer asking for the first question, the answers it is to accept as correct, and the feedback it is to give when the student answers correctly:

Enter question number 1

Which is the largest state?

Enter correct answers

Alas

Enter correct feedback

That's right. Alaska is the largest state.

The authoring system will accept as correct any answer that contains the string of letters given as the correct answer. Mr. Stevenson used *Alas* so that the computer would accept common misspellings of Alaska, such as Alasca. As long as the student enters an answer that contains the sequence of letters *Alas* he will be given credit for a correct response.

The authoring system also makes it easy to check for common incorrect answers and to give the student specific feedback:

Enter wrong answers, set number 1:

Calif, New York,NY,N.Y.

Enter feedback for wrong answers, set number 1:

No. That is a large state with a lot of people, but it is not the largest state.

Enter wrong answers, set number 2:

Texas

Enter feedback for wrong answers, set number 2:

No. That is a large state, but it is not the largest of all 50 states.

Enter wrong answers, set number 3:

— — (Specifies any answer other than those already given)

Enter wrong feedback, set number 3:

No, that is not the largest state.

Mr. Stevenson also sets the number of chances each student will be given, and he enters a hint and the feedback message for students who do not answer the question correctly:

Enter number of chances to be given:

2

Enter hint to be given after first error:

It was one of the last states to join the United States.

Enter feedback for incorrect answer on final try:

No. Alaska is the largest state.

Enter question number 2:

Do you know which state is the smallest one?

Mr. Stevenson continued entering the rest of his lesson. Here are some sample dialogues between the computer and students using Mr. Stevenson's lesson:

Dialogue #1

This lesson is about U.S. geography. First, I'm going to ask you some questions to find out how much you already know. Which is the largest state?

Alasska. It's even bigger than Texas

That's right, Alaska is the largest state.
Do you know which state is the smallest one?
...

Dialogue #2

This lesson is about U.S. geography. First, I'm going to ask you some questions to find out how much you already know. Which is the largest state?

N.Y.

No. That is a large state with a lot of people, but it is not the largest state in size.
Please try again.
Hint: It was one of the last states to join the United States.

Hawaii

No. Alaska is the largest state.
Do you know which state is the smallest one?
...

Dialogue #3

This lesson is about U.S. geography. First, I'm going to ask you some questions to find out how much you already know. Which is the largest state?

Texas

No. That is a big state, but it's not the largest of all 50 states.
Please try again.
Hint: It was one of the last states to join the United States.

Alasca

That's right. Alaska is the largest state.
Do you know which is the smallest state?
...

In these dialogues, the computer gives intelligent-appearing responses to the students' answers. In dialogue #1, the computer recognizes the correct answer even though it is misspelled and another state is named in the same sentence. In the other two dialogues, the computer gives reasonable responses to the students' incorrect answers, and it gives hints and second chances. It also recognizes the abbreviation N.Y. and another misspelling of Alaska.

Although the program can make the computer appear to carry on an intelligent dialogue, the computer has no knowledge of its own. The person who creates the lesson must tell the computer appropriate responses for each answer students might give. Mr. Stevenson demonstrated how unexpected answers can show that the computer lacks any knowledge of its own, but simply does exactly what it has been told. He took the part of the student in the following interchange:

Dialogue #4

This lesson is about U.S. geography. First I'm going to ask you some questions to find out how much you already know. Which is the largest state?

Alas, I wish I knew

That's right. Alaska is the largest state.
Do you know which is the smallest state?
...

The computer seems to have accepted the answer "Alas, I wish I knew" as correct. This is because it had been instructed to accept any word that begins with the letters ALAS as correct, so students would be given credit for close misspellings such as *Alasca*. The computer, following its instructions, accepts any answer starting with these letters, regardless of how obvious it would be to a person that the student does not know the answer. That is, the intelligent-appearing responses of the computer depend completely upon whether the person who created the lesson provided appropriate responses for all the answers students might give. Whether or not a computerized lesson takes good advantage of the potential strengths of computers depends completely upon the quality of the lesson program.

Chapter 8

Computerized Drill and Practice

Practice is necessary to become proficient at any skill, whether it is a physical skill such as bicycling or a mental skill such as reading. In almost every school, teachers and students devote a great deal of time and effort to practice drills in math, reading, spelling and other areas. Computers with well-designed software can make many of these drills more effective and enjoyable. However, there are controversies about the role of drill and practice in schools, and whether computers should be used for this purpose.

One controversy centers on the amount of time and effort that should be devoted to drill work. Some educators view drills as primarily busy work, designed to occupy children's time, not help them develop useful abilities. They believe students should spend their time in activities that involve more thought and exploration, and they advocate that computers be reserved for such activities.

Another controversy centers on the nature of the practice exercises given to students. Many educators believe that common approaches to reading, math and other drills are ineffective, perhaps even detrimental. Often, this debate concerns the virtues of dividing skills into many subskills and having students practice each one in isolation, as opposed to practicing the entire skill at once. The most common example is in the teaching of reading, where the contrast is between emphasizing phonics and word recognition subskills versus emphasizing practice in reading real books, magazines and newspapers.

Ms. Byron explained that drill and practice was the first use of computers at Babbage School. Some of the early drill programs were poorly designed, but once the teachers obtained good programs they found computerized drills to be very effective. As teachers and students became more comfortable with computers, they began to learn about other ways computers can be used. Drill and practice is now just one of many applications of computers, but the teachers regard it as a valuable one. Ms. Byron emphasized that:

> Practice is necessary for many skills, and computers can make practice drills more effective. At Babbage School, we use drill programs in teaching typing, math, spelling, reading, music and sign language. These programs enable students to master skills more quickly and they spare teachers the tedium of creating, monitoring and checking drill work. The use of computers for drill and practice thereby gives students and teachers additional time to engage in more conceptual, exploratory and creative activities.

Most drills follow a similar format. Practice items, such as math problems or typing sequences, are presented. Students respond to each item, answering questions or performing actions. At some point, they receive feedback about the accuracy of their work. For some skills, students also receive feedback about their speed. After they receive feedback, students are given additional practice on those items with which they had difficulty.

WHAT MAKES DRILLS EFFECTIVE?

Several factors determine the effectiveness of practice. First, the selection of the practice items is critical. There is no value in having students practice items they have already mastered or cannot handle at all. Drills that are too easy result in boredom; drills that are too difficult result in frustration rather than learning.

Another important factor in making practice effective is the nature of the feedback and how quickly it is provided. Feedback should do more that simply tell students whether they are right or wrong; it should help them understand and correct their mistakes. For example, it does not help to tell students that $2+2$ is not 5 unless they are led to understand that $2+2$ equals 4 and $2+3$ equals 5. In addition, it is best for students to receive feedback immediately after they make responses. Immediate feedback enables them to catch their errors and learn the correct responses while they are still actively involved in the drill. It also prevents them from repeating the same mistakes, and it helps keep their attention on their work. For skills in which speed is important, immediate feedback helps students know when their speed is lagging and when it is increasing.

Drills can also be made more effective by making them more enjoyable. Incorporating drills into games increases the likelihood that students will devote sufficient time and attention to practicing the skill.

Computers can be programmed to present practice items, monitor students' performance, adjust the items to an appropriate level for each individual, and provide immediate feedback to help students understand and correct their errors. For skills in which speed is important, computers can report the time of every response and control how quickly practice items are presented. Drills can also be incorporated into computer games that hold students' interest.

Most students prefer computerized drills to other types. They like the fact that computers always wait until they are ready and repeat the practice items as often as necessary. They also like being told immediately whether they are correct, without having to wait for the teacher to check their work. Students generally find negative feedback from the computer to be less upsetting than negative feedback from teachers. In timed drills, students like to race against the clock to see if they can do the drill faster than they have before. They particularly enjoy the programs that turn the drills into games.

TYPING DRILLS

All the students at Babbage School use computer programs to help them master typing skills. They first receive instructions from a teacher about the value of touch typing, the home position for their fingers, and how to properly strike each key. Then they use a typing drill program that has three parts. The first part teaches the location of each key, the second part helps increase typing speed, and the third part administers and scores typing tests.

The program begins by drilling the student on the locations of the four home keys for the left hand. It presents different combinations of these letters for the student to type—ASDF, FSDA, DAFS, and so on. When the student presses an incorrect key, the computer sounds a tone, so the student immediately recognizes and corrects the mistake. The program continues with the first four keys until the student correctly types 10 consecutive sequences. It then adds the four home keys for the right hand and, when the student masters these, continues to gradually add keys until the student has mastered them all.

After the student has learned the location of all the keys, he begins more advanced drills that improve his typing speed. In this part of the program, the computer presents words for the student to type, and it monitors the speed and accuracy of each key stroke. The program analyzes the student's typing and gives extra practice on those letters and sequences he typed slowly or incorrectly. For example, if the computer detects that the student is weak on the *ea* sequence, it will give him practice words such as *each, beach, early* and *wear*. With this continuous adjusting of the drill items, every student spends most of his practice time on exactly those keys and sequences on which he needs the most practice. This dynamic adjusting of practice items can be accomplished only with a computer.

The third part of the program presents paragraphs for typing tests. The computer automatically scores the tests and reports the number of errors, the letters typed incorrectly, and the typing speed.

These computerized typing drills have several advantages over typing drills from books. During learning, the computer immediately signals when an error is made, so incorrect typing habits do not become ingrained. The computer also saves students and teachers the effort of checking for errors and measuring typing speed. Most importantly, by continuously checking students' typing and creating drills tailored to each individual, the computer enables students to make the best possible use of the time they spend practicing.

A typing drill game, called *Mastertype*™, is also used by students at Babbage School. In this game, the player defends his planet against attackers from a planet called Lexicon. The attackers appear at the four corners of the screen and move toward the planet while firing missiles. In each corner, there is a word or letter sequence (see Figure 8.1). The player must destroy the attackers by quickly and accurately typing each of the words or letter sequences. If he types too slowly or makes too many errors, the planet will be destroyed and he loses the game.

The Mastertype program has a series of levels. The sequences at the early levels just use the letters on the middle row of keys (ASDFGHJKL). As the student advances to higher levels, other letters are added, and then longer, more difficult words. The speed of the attackers approaching the planet also increases. With the

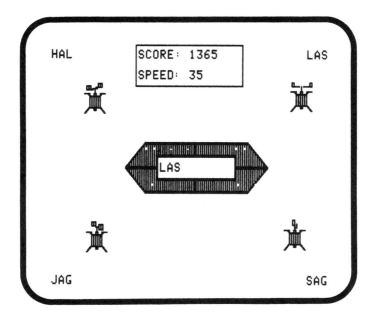

FIGURE 8.1 Mastertype program display.

arcade-like graphics and sounds of this program, many students get so caught up in the game they forget they are actually involved in the drudgery of typing practice.

MATH DRILLS

Computerized math drills are used for all grade levels at Babbage School. There are a large variety of programs available, covering the entire range from simple addition to algebra. Some programs incorporate math drills into arcade-like games. A screen display from a math game is shown in Figure 8.2. The game, called *Meteor Multiplication*™, is similar in concept to the Mastertype program just described. In this program, the student turns his laser gun toward a meteor and then types the answer to the problem written on that meteor. If he is correct, the meteor is destroyed. He has to work quickly and accurately to prevent any meteors from reaching and damaging the space station. Similar games are used for addition, subtraction and division facts.

Other math drill programs use formats more like standard paper-and-pencil drills. Although not as much fun as the game pro-

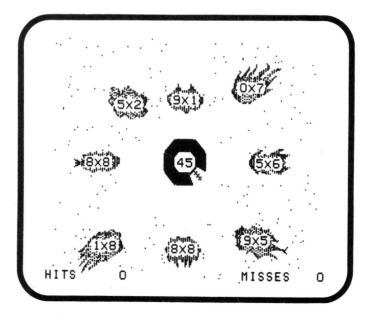

FIGURE 8.2   *Meteor Multiplication* program display.

grams, these programs have certain advantages. They allow the student to actually work the problem on the computer screen and are therefore suitable for a wider range of difficulty levels. They also provide more helpful feedback than the game programs.

Doris, a third-grade student, has been using an addition drill program that can create problems at twelve different levels of difficulty. The easiest problems have two numbers, each with one digit. The most difficult problems have five numbers, each with seven digits. Every time a student uses this program, it creates a new set of problems. Students work the problems directly on the computer screen, without any need for paper and pencil.

Doris had successfully answered problems at the first five levels, and so she starts at level six. The computer displays one problem at a time on the screen. Doris enters her answers by typing the appropriate numbers, working from right to left (as she would with paper-and-pencil). A special key lets her erase, and she can mark carrying or regrouping by holding down the shift key while typing a number. When she finishes answering a problem, she presses the RETURN key and the computer tells her whether her answer was correct. Figure 8.3 shows the computer screen display after Doris entered a correct answer.

Figure 8.4 shows the display after Doris answered a problem incorrectly. The program was set to give her only one chance, so

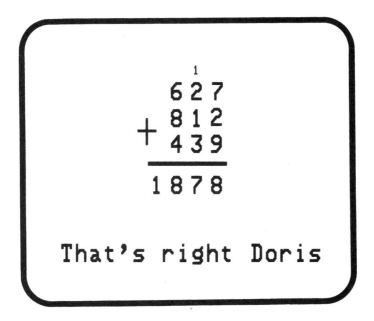

FIGURE 8.3 Math drill program response to a correct answer.

the computer displayed the correct answer. Doris pointed out that the computer shows the correct answer lined up with her incorrect one, so she can compare them easily and find her mistake.

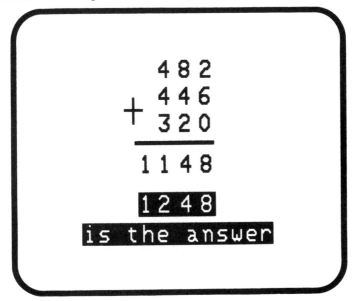

FIGURE 8.4 Math drill program response to an incorrect answer.

Doris explained that after every ten problems the program reports how many of her answers were correct. If she gets all ten correct, she goes on to the next level. If she gets fewer than seven correct, the program takes her back to an easier level. She also pointed out that the teacher can set the program to give her a second or third chance when she makes a mistake.

This math drill program has several advantages over workbooks or problem sheets. The computer generates the problems and checks students' work, thereby saving teachers' time. The program gives each student problems at an appropriate level of difficulty, and it allows each individual to work at his own speed. The immediate positive feedback rewards students for correct answers; the immediate negative feedback helps them learn from their mistakes. Problems answered incorrectly are presented again later on, so students get more practice on problems that gave them difficulty. In addition, students enjoy working on the computer more than with paper and pencil. They like the immediate feedback and being able to change the level of difficulty after each set of ten problems. They also like the fact that the computer lets them erase and correct their answers without making a mess. As one student said, "I can erase all I want without making a hole in the computer screen like I do on paper."

SPELLING DRILLS

The spelling drill program used at Babbage School works in conjunction with an audio tape recorder connected to the computer. The teacher selects a list of words, types the words into the computer, and makes a tape recording with a message for each word. When making a tape, the teacher usually says the word, gives a sentence with it, and then repeats the word. Once this is done for a word list, any number of children can use it.

Marlene is a fourth-grade student who likes to use the computer to help her learn spelling words. When she begins the program, the computer displays a message telling her to put the tape into the recorder, rewind it, press the PLAY button, and then press the RETURN key so the computer knows she is ready for the first word. She does so and the tape plays the message recorded by the teacher for the first word: "The first word is recipe. I have a delicious cake recipe. Spell *recipe*." The computer then waits for Marlene to type the word. She spells it correctly, and the computer displays a congratulatory message.

The computer then starts the tape to play the next message: "The second word is *receive*. I hope to receive many presents for my birthday. Receive." The tape then stops and Marlene types the word, but she spells it incorrectly. The program shows her which letters were correct and gives her another chance on the letters she missed (see Figure 8.5). However, Marlene again makes an error. The computer then displays the correct spelling, with the letters she had missed highlighted (see Figure 8.6). The program lets Marlene study the correct spelling as long as she wants. When Marlene presses RETURN, the computer clears the screen and waits for her to type the word again. It does not let her go on until she spells the word correctly.

This program helps students recognize their errors and work to correct them—something they are unlikely to do when they take a standard spelling quiz and do not receive feedback until the next day. The feedback is designed to help children focus their attention on the correct spelling and, in particular, those letters they had missed. One teacher explained that this attention-directing feature, combined with the requirement that students spell the entire word correctly before continuing, makes this program especially valuable for children who are poor spellers and have trouble learning words on their own.

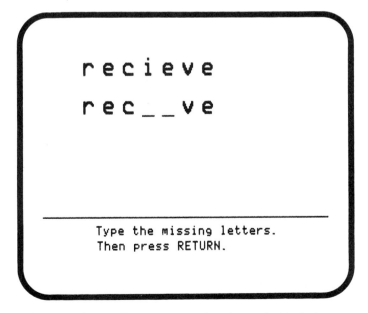

FIGURE 8.5 The spelling program after the student's first error.

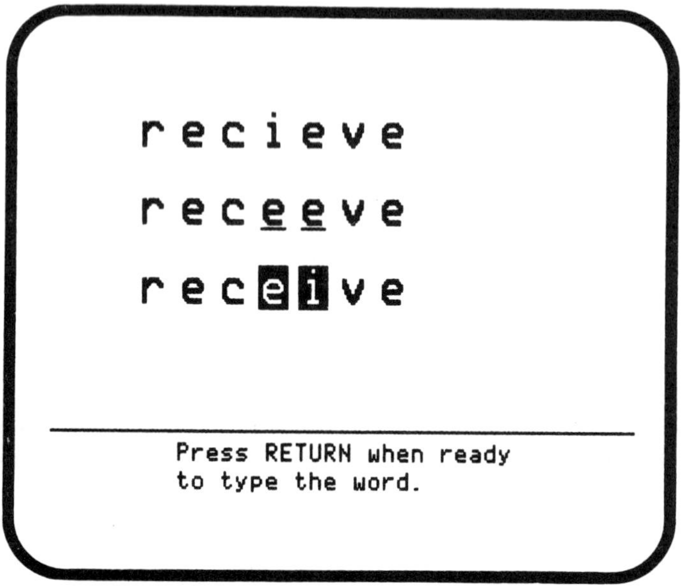

```
          r e c i e v e

          r e c e e v e

          r e c e i v e


      ─────────────────────────

          Press RETURN when ready
          to type the word.
```

FIGURE 8.6   The spelling program after the student made a second error on the word.

READING DRILLS

There are a wide variety of computerized reading drills that give students practice in word recognition, sentence understanding and story comprehension.

One word recognition drill makes use of the computer's capability to display a word for a brief period of time. A word flashes quickly on the screen, and the student tries to recognize and type it. The computer adjusts the length of time the words are exposed, increasing the time when students fail to recognize words and decreasing it when they succeed. As a student advances in the drill, the computer also selects longer, more difficult words to be displayed.

In a variation of this drill, the student hears a word played on a tape recorder (with the same arrangment as used in the spelling drill). Words then flash, one at a time, on the computer screen. The student presses a key when he recognizes the word he heard. This same drill can be adapted so the student presses the key when he sees a synonym or antonym of the word. This gives students practice working with the meanings of words, not just the letters.

Another reading drill gives students practice in understanding the correspondence between pictures and sentences. The computer displays animated pictures and sentences. For each picture-sentence pair, the student types *yes* if the sentence fits the picture and *no* if it does not. If the answer is *no*, the child changes the sentence to make it fit. For example, a simple animation shows a boy throwing a red ball, and the sentence reads:

The boy throws a green ball.

The child should then respond *no* and retype the sentence with the word *red* replacing *green*. This program has a variety of levels of difficulty that the teacher or student can choose.

There is also a drill program that uses the *cloze procedure* commonly found in reading workbooks and exams. In this procedure, students are given a written passage in which certain words have been replaced by blanks. They fill in appropriate words as they read the passage. The cloze procedure taps students' understanding of the passage, and it gives them practice using context to figure out words. However, there is one serious weakness with it as used in workbooks: A single mistake at the beginning of a passage may lead a student to make many mistakes later on. That is, if the student misconstrues the beginning of the passage, he may never be able to get back on the right track. The computer program avoids this problem. It provides students with immediate feedback for each answer. When a student is incorrect, the computer gives him another chance and then, if necessary, gives the correct answer. Therefore the student cannot proceed with the passage until he has seen the correct word.

Other reading drills are designed to practice extracting main ideas and drawing inferences from written passages. These drills present passages and ask questions, just like standard reading tests. However, when the student answers a question incorrectly, the program shows the passage again and has the student search for information relevant to the question. If the student needs help, the program will highlight key words and phrases on the computer screen, thereby helping the student locate where in the text the relevant information is found.

MUSIC DRILLS

Computerized drills are also used in music classes at Babbage School. For example, one music drill helps students learn to match written notes with melodies. The student sees written notes on the computer screen and then hears notes played. One of the notes played does not match the corresponding written note. The student's job is to identify the incorrect note. He can have the computer repeat the melody as many times as he wants before giving

FIGURE 8.7 Music drill program. A melody has been played in which one note does not match the written sequence.

FIGURE 8.8 Music drill program. When the student answers incorrectly, the program shows the notes of the melody actually played.

136

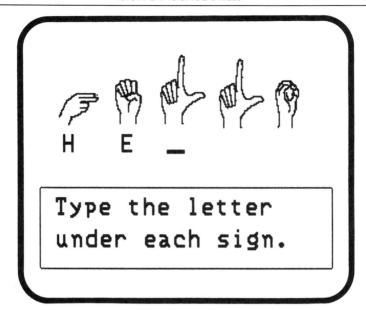

FIGURE 8.9   Finger spelling drill. The word is "HELLO".

his answer (see Figure 8.7). If the student answers correctly, the program goes on to the next set of notes. If the student answers incorrectly, the program shows the written version of the notes played, so the student can see where the mismatch occurred. It also lets the student play both the melody of the original written notes and the mismatching melody (see Figure 8.8).

SIGN LANGUAGE DRILLS

Some of the students at Babbage School take a special class in sign language. They use a computer program that gives them practice in recognizing common signs and reading finger spelling. The program shows illustrations of hands on the screen. Students interpret the word or phrase and type it into the computer. Figure 8.9 shows an example of a finger spelling drill.

In sign language, the direction of movements is often as important as the position of the hands. The computer drill program therefore includes animated sequences. It can also vary the speed in which it displays sequences of signs, so students can work to increase the speed at which they can interpret them. Furthermore, when students mistake one sign for another, the program can display the two signs side-by-side, so they can see the difference. The students find these drills to be very helpful in learning to understand sign language.

CONCLUSION

Computers can facillitate many types of drills. They can present practice items, monitor students' performance, adjust the drills to be appropriate for each individual and provide immediate and helpful feedback. Computers can make mastering skills more efficient and enjoyable for students, and they can save teachers time and effort in preparing, monitoring and checking drill work.

Chapter 9

Learning to Program

Computers are obedient servants, useful in education, business and recreation. However, to do anything at all, computers must be given step-by-step instructions. That is, they must be programmed.

Programs are available to make computers perform a wide variety of functions. Therefore, most people who use computers do not write their own programs, and, in fact, do not need to know how to program at all. However, there are several benefits to learning to program. By learning to program, students acquire a better understanding of the nature of computers, their capabilities and limitations. Programming also helps students develop their thinking and problem solving skills, as well as careful, systematic work habits. In addition, many students find controlling a computer with their own programs to be fun and exciting.

THE NATURE OF COMPUTER PROGRAMS

Computer programs are often said to be similar to recipes in that both consist of sequences of instructions. However, instructions for computers must be far more detailed and exact than recipes or other instructions for people. Computers need to be told everything they are to do and how to do each thing. They will follow instructions that any person would recognize as inappropriate, and they cannot interpret vague instructions nor rely upon knowledge gained from prior experiences. For example, suppose you had a computer-controlled robot and wanted to program it to add an egg to a recipe. You would have to instruct it to find and recognize an egg, crack it open, discard the shell, and mix the white and yolk with the other ingredients. You would even have to tell it how vigorously to mix the ingredients and for how long. If your instructions were not sufficiently explicit, the robot might select an avocado or even a cup instead of an egg. Or if you mistakenly instructed it to crack the egg and then add it to the other ingredients, the robot would add the cracked shell along with the rest of the egg.

Computer programs must be written in a language the computer can process. Later in this chapter, there are example programs written in BASIC and in Logo, the two languages most commonly used with personal computers in education. There are many other programming languages, such as Pascal, PILOT, Fortran, Cobol, Algol, APL, Ada, Forth and Lisp. Each language is best suited for certain types of programs. For example, Cobol is primarily for business applications while Fortran is primarily for mathematics and engineering applications. BASIC and Logo are well suited for teaching children to program.

BASIC, Logo, and the other languages listed are *high level languages*. High level languages are designed to make programming as easy as possible. Most commands in these languages are English words, and the programs are organized in ways that are reasonably natural for people to follow and understand. Within the computer, high level languages are translated to a numeric *machine language*. This happens automatically, so programmers working with high level languages do not need to know machine language. (For interested readers, machine language is described in Appendix A.)

While the commands in high level programming languages are generally English words, computers cannot understand normal English. Each instruction in a computer program must be exact in both form and function. A person will usually understand instructions despite misspelled words or incorrect punctuation, but a computer cannot follow instructions unless they conform exactly to the rules of the programming language. For example, if we command a computer that uses BASIC to:

PRINT "HELLO"

it will obey and print on the display screen:

HELLO

However, if we accidently type the command as:

PRUNT "HELLO"

The computer will respond with:

SYNTAX ERROR

Likewise, if we tried:

WRITE "HELLO"

the computer would again respond:

SYNTAX ERROR

PRINT is a command in the BASIC language, but PRUNT and WRITE are not.

WRITING SIMPLE PROGRAMS IN BASIC

When Jillian and Denny, two sixth graders at Babbage School, began working on their first program, they chose a simple goal, to convert meters to feet. Then, they followed the four steps in creating a program their teacher had recommended: *designing, coding, testing* and *debugging*. Designing the program means dividing the overall goal into simpler subgoals, and figuring out the order and organization of the subgoals. Coding is translating each subgoal into commands written in the programming language. Testing refers to checking that the program does everything correctly, and debugging refers to finding and correcting errors (which programmers call *bugs*).

In designing their program, Jillian and Denny agreed it should be divided into five simple substeps. They wrote these down:

1. Print a message telling the user to enter the number of meters.

2. Have the computer wait for the person to enter the number of meters.

3. Use the formula Feet = Meters × 3.28.

4. Print the answer.

5. Go back to step 1 and start over.

They then coded these five steps into commands in the BASIC language. Here is their program:

```
100 PRINT "HOW MANY METERS?"
110 INPUT M
120 F = M * 3.28
130 PRINT "IN FEET, THAT IS EQUAL TO " F
140 GOTO 100
```

In this simple program, each line corresponds to one substep of the design. (In more complex programs, multiple lines might be required for single substeps of the design.)

Each line of a BASIC program is given a number. Jillian and Denny followed their teacher's suggestion to begin at number 100 and add at least 10 for the number of each successive line. This leaves space for them to add additional commands at the beginning of the program and, if necessary, between lines.

In Jillian and Denny's program, the PRINT command in line 100 tells the computer to print the "HOW MANY METERS?" message on the display screen. The INPUT command in line 110 tells the computer to wait until an answer is typed on the keyboard and the RETURN key is pressed. The M after INPUT instructs the computer to store the number typed in a *variable* called M.

Variables are used to save information to be used later. You can think of variables as boxes within the computer's memory. The name of the variable (M in this case) is like a label on the box. The value of M is the contents of the box. For example, if the person using the program answered "12," the number 12 would be stored in the variable M. Later in the program, the computer could check what is stored in M, and it would find the number 12.

Line 120 is a way of representing in BASIC the formula Feet = Meters × 3.28. It instructs the computer to check the value stored in M, multiply it by 3.28, and store the result in variable F. If M is equal to 12, then 39.36 (the result of 12 × 3.28) would be stored in F.

Line 130 contains another PRINT command. The computer prints anything placed between quotes exactly as it appears, so it will print *IN FEET, THAT IS EQUAL TO* . However, the letter F is outside the quotes. This tells the computer that F is a variable. When it encounters a variable in a PRINT command, the computer prints the value of the variable. In our example, line 130 would cause the computer to print:

IN FEET, THAT IS EQUAL TO 39.36

Line 140 simply tells the computer to go back to line 100 and start again from the beginning. The computer will repeat the program until it is turned off or a special RESET key is pressed. Each time the program is repeated, the value of variable M will be replaced by the new value entered, and the value of F will be replaced by the new value calculated in the program.

Jillian and Denny tested their program by entering different numbers and checking the computer's answer with a calculator. They were happy to find the program worked perfectly. They then decided to expand it to convert feet to meters as well as meters to feet. They worked on the design for this more advanced program and agreed upon the following steps:

1. Print a message asking whether the program should convert feet-to-meters or meters-to-feet.

2. Wait for the answer. Store it in variable U (for units).

3. If meters-to-feet is selected then:

   a. Print a message asking how many meters.

   b. Wait for the answer. Store it in variable M (for meters).

   c. Calculate the number of feet using the formula Feet = Meters × 3.28. Store the answer in variable F (for feet).

   d. Print the answer.

   e. Go back to step 1 and start over.

4. If feet-to-meters is selected then:

   a. Print a message asking how many feet.

   b. Wait for the answer. Store it in variable F (for feet).

   c. Calculate the number of meters using the formula Meters = Feet × 3.28. Store the answer in variable M (for meters).

   d. Print the answer.

   e. Go back to step 1 and start over.

Then, they coded the program into BASIC:

```
100 PRINT "TYPE 1 TO START WITH METERS OR 2 TO START WITH FEET"
110 INPUT U
120 IF U = 1 THEN GOTO 200
130 IF U = 2 THEN GOTO 300
200 PRINT "HOW MANY METERS?"
210 INPUT M
220 F = M * 3.28
230 PRINT "IN FEET, THAT IS EQUAL TO " F
300 PRINT "HOW MANY FEET?"
310 INPUT F
320 M = F / 3.28
330 PRINT "IN METERS, THAT IS EQUAL TO " M
340 GOTO 100
```

Line 100 contains a PRINT command and line 110 contains an INPUT command. Both types of commands have already been described. Line 120 contains a new type of command, IF/THEN. This is a *conditional* statement. IF the condition (U = 1) is true, THEN the computer will perform the action (go to line 200). If the condition is false, the computer will not perform the action but will continue with the command on the next line. Line 130 also contains an IF/THEN instruction, but with a different condition (U = 2) and action (GOTO 300).

Jillian and Denny began the commands for converting meters to feet at line 200. These commands are identical to those in the previous program. They began the commands for converting feet to meters at line 300. The IF/THEN commands in lines 120 and 130 make the computer *branch* to the appropriate line, depending upon how the user of the program answered the first question.

Line 340 sends the computer back to line 100, so the entire program repeats.

The students tested their new program. When they tried to convert feet to meters, the program properly printed the answer and returned to the first question:

TYPE 1 TO START WITH METERS OR 2 TO START WITH FEET
2
HOW MANY FEET?
100
IN METERS, THAT IS EQUAL TO 30.4878049
TYPE 1 TO START WITH METERS OR 2 TO START WITH FEET
1

When they tried to convert meters to feet, the program did the conversion and printed the answer correctly, but did not return to the first question. Continuing from the previous interaction with the computer:

HOW MANY METERS?
500
IN FEET, THAT IS EQUAL TO 1640
HOW MANY FEET?

Jillian and Denny realized something was wrong. After the computer converted a number, it was supposed to return to the beginning of the program and again ask whether they wanted to start with meters or feet. However, after it converted 500 meters to 1,640 feet, it did not go back to the right command. It seemed to assume they would start with feet. Denny was upset that their program did not work correctly, but Jillian reminded him of the sign on the classroom wall: "Don't worry, computer bugs don't byte."

They carefully examined their program and discovered they had left out a command. When the computer completes one command, it goes to the next one in order, unless there is a GOTO (or other branch command). In Jillian and Denny's program, after the computer changed meters to feet (line 220) and printed the answer (line 230), they wanted it to return to line 100. However, they forgot to put in a command for the computer to do so. It therefore continued on to the next line, 300. To fix this bug, they simply added the needed command in line 240. Here is their revised program:

```
100 PRINT "TYPE 1 TO START WITH METERS OR 2 TO START WITH FEET"
110 INPUT U
120 IF U = 1 THEN GOTO 200
130 IF U = 2 THEN GOTO 300
200 PRINT "HOW MANY METERS?"
210 INPUT M
220 F = M * 3.28
230 PRINT "IN FEET, THAT IS EQUAL TO " F
240 GOTO 100
300 PRINT "HOW MANY FEET?"
310 INPUT F
320 M = F / 3.28
330 PRINT "IN METERS, THAT IS EQUAL TO " M
340 GOTO 100
```

They tested this program and were pleased to find it worked perfectly. They excitedly began working on the next extension to their program, to make it convert kilograms to pounds and pounds to kilograms.

WRITING SIMPLE PROGRAMS IN LOGO

Logo is a newer programming language than BASIC. It is becoming popular, particularly for use by children. Logo programs are organized very differently than BASIC programs, and Logo has certain advantages as a first language for children to learn.

The best known feature of Logo is the set of commands for creating pictures on the computer screen. These commands, known as *turtle graphics* commands, are used in the examples below. The name "turtle graphics" comes from an early computer system that controlled the movements of a robot shaped somewhat like a turtle. This computer system could be used to program the turtle-robot to move and draw.

In most current systems, the turtle is just a marker on the computer screen, but the same types of commands are used as with the turtle-robot. Simple commands tell the screen turtle to move forward or backward a number of steps, turn left or right a number of degrees, select a pen of a certain color, and raise or lower the pen to control whether the turtle draws a trail as it moves.

Figure 9.1 shows the results of some commands to the turtle. Part A shows the turtle, which is represented on the screen by a triangle. The filled part marks the front of the turtle, so you can tell which way it is facing. Part B shows the screen after the turtle has been given the command FORWARD 100. The turtle has moved forward 100 turtle steps, leaving a trail as it moved (i.e., the turtle's pen is down). Part C shows the effect of the command RIGHT 90. The turtle has turned right 90 degrees (i.e., one quarter of a full rotation). RIGHT changes the direction the turtle is facing, but does not move the turtle from its current location. The remaining parts of Figure 9.1 show the effects of other FORWARD and RIGHT commands.

Within a Logo program, commands are grouped into *procedures*. Each procedure instructs the computer to perform a series of actions. For example, here is a procedure for drawing a square with sides that are 100 turtle steps long:

```
TO SQUARE
  FORWARD 100
  RIGHT 90
  FORWARD 100
  RIGHT 90
  FORWARD 100
  RIGHT 90
  FORWARD 100
END
```

Creating a procedure is like teaching the computer a new word. In this procedure, the first line tells the computer that we are going to teach it TO SQUARE. We can give a procedure any name, but it's best to choose a name that describes what the procedure does. The

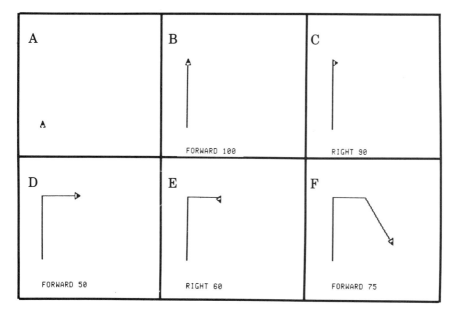

FIGURE 9.1   Examples of turtle graphics commands.

last line simply ends the procedure. In between are the commands for the turtle to follow when told to SQUARE – go 100 steps forward and turn right, four successive times.

Once this procedure is entered into the computer, we can use SQUARE just as if it were one of the commands built into the language, such as FORWARD or RIGHT. That is, the one word SQUARE will direct the turtle to follow all the instructions in the procedure. After a procedure has been created, it can stand as an independent unit or be combined in various ways with other procedures. Sophisticated programs are built by combining simple procedures into progressively more powerful ones.

Turtle graphics procedures are easy to test and debug, since you can see whether the turtle did as you expected. For example, a common first attempt to write a TRIANGLE procedure is:

```
TO TRIANGLE
    FORWARD 50
    RIGHT 60
    FORWARD 50
    RIGHT 60
    FORWARD 50
END
```

The result of this program is shown in Figure 9.2.

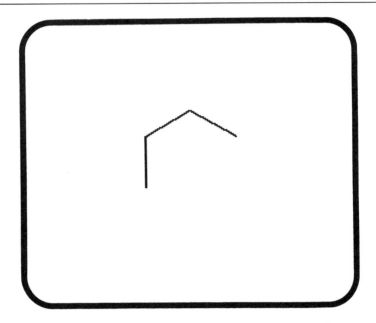

FIGURE 9.2   A first attempt to create a TRIANGLE procedure.

This program clearly contains a bug. The problem is in the number of degrees the turtle has been told to turn. While it is correct that each angle of an equilateral triangle is 60 degrees, these are the inside angles. The turtle must traverse the outside angles, each of which is 120 degrees. Another way to think about it is the turtle must turn more at each corner to draw an equilateral triangle than to draw a square. Therefore the correct program is (see Figure 9.3):

```
TO TRIANGLE
  FORWARD 50
  RIGHT 120
  FORWARD 50
  RIGHT 120
  FORWARD 50
END
```

When we want the computer to repeat a series of actions, it becomes tedious to retype all the commands many times. Fortunately, Logo provides a simple way of telling the computer to repeat commands. For example, the TRIANGLE procedure could be shortened to:

```
TO TRIANGLE
  REPEAT 3 [FORWARD 50 RIGHT 120]
END
```

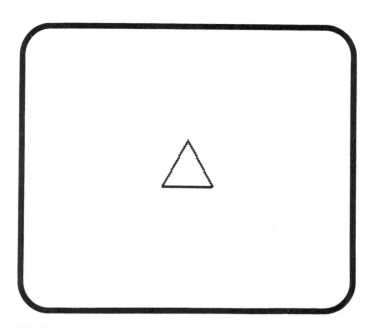

FIGURE 9.3   The result of the corrected TRIANGLE procedure.

REPEAT tells the turtle to do the commands within the brackets the number of times specified. An octagon would be created by (see Figure 9.4):

```
TO OCTAGON
  REPEAT 8 [FORWARD 60 RIGHT 45]
END
```

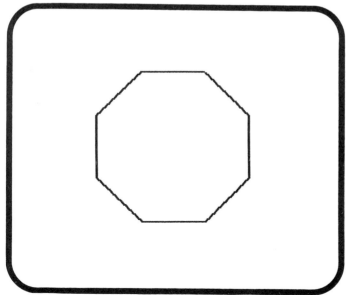

FIGURE 9.4   The result of the OCTOGON procedure.

If you examine the procedures for the triangle, square and octagon, you will see that the total amount of turning for each is 360 degrees. The fact that a closed figure requires 360 degrees is called (in the world of turtle graphics) the *Total Turtle Trip Theorem*. This theorem provides the principle needed to get the turtle to draw a closed shape with any number of sides. It is also an example of how programming can lead children to learn things in other areas— geometry in this case.

We might also want to draw squares of different sizes. Rather than have a separate procedure for each size, it would be more efficient to have one general procedure that lets us vary the size. That is, we want a procedure in which the number of steps the turtle moves for each side is a variable that can be changed. We can call the variable :SIZE (the colon before a word signifies that it is a variable in Logo). Here is the procedure:

```
TO SQUARE :SIZE
  REPEAT 4 [FORWARD :SIZE RIGHT 90]
END
```

:SIZE in the first line tells the turtle that this procedure uses a variable called :SIZE. We then tell the turtle the meaning of SQUARE, using the variable :SIZE for how many steps the turtle will move forward. Once we have created this procedure we can use SQUARE anytime we want, telling the computer what value we want to give the variable :SIZE. For example, we can tell the turtle:

```
SQUARE 5
SQUARE 10
SQUARE 15
SQUARE 25
SQUARE 40
SQUARE 65
SQUARE 105
SQUARE 170
```

and obtain the picture shown in Figure 9.5.

Turtle graphics makes it easy to create interesting patterns. Figure 9.6 shows three pictures created by repeated combinations of SQUARE and RIGHT. The capability to create your own procedures, such as we did with SQUARE, and then easily use them as building blocks in more complex procedures, is one of the major advantages of the Logo language.

Turtle graphics is just one part of the full Logo language. The other important part consists of *list processing* commands used to write programs that operate upon words rather than pictures. List

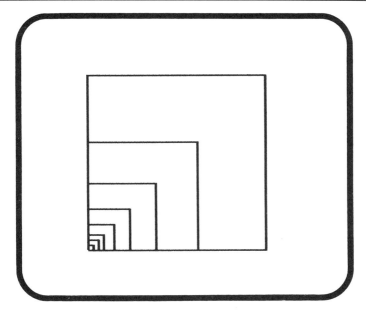

FIGURE 9.5 A picture created by using the SQUARE procedure eight times, with a different value given to :SIZE each time.

processing commands let you program the computer to do things such as check whether a word is contained in a list of words or select the first and last words of a sentence. List processing commands are grouped into procedures, just like turtle graphics commands, and the two types of commands are often combined in a single program.

BENEFITS OF LEARNING TO PROGRAM

The teachers at Babbage School believe every student should learn the fundamentals of programming. All students are required to take an introductory programming class. Many students also choose to take optional advanced classes, and some have formed a computer programming club. In the club, students work together on programming projects, learning a great deal from each other and from their collaborative problem solving efforts. In fact, the best programmers at Babbage School are not teachers, but some of the students in the programming club.

Ms. Byron explained the benefits of students learning to write programs. First of all, they gain a better understanding of the capabilities and limitations of computers. Once students have written their own programs, they realize that computers are not the magical, all-powerful machines described in science fiction stories. They understand that computers are tools that have to be guided

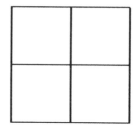

A. REPEAT 4 [SQUARE 75 RIGHT 90].

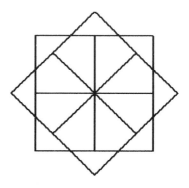

B. REPEAT 8 [SQUARE 75 RIGHT 45].

C. REPEAT 20 [SQUARE 75 RIGHT 18].

FIGURE 9.6 Three pictures created with REPEAT, SQUARE and RIGHT.

and directed by people. Learning about programming is part of becoming "computer literate."

Since computers and programming are such important parts of our society, Ms. Byron believes all students should have some experience with them. She realizes most students will not become programmers, but explained:

> We also encourage each student to try painting, writing, acting, playing musical instruments, performing scientific experiments, and many other activities. We believe schools should expose students to as wide a range of experiences as possible. That way, children find out where their interests and talents lie. Only a few children will ever work as professional programmers, or even program occasionally for their job or as a hobby. But they will all benefit from understanding the nature of programming and experiencing what it is like to create their own programs.

Ms. Byron continued to explain another benefit of programming: It helps children develop their thinking and problem solving abilities. She has found that children often use techniques they are taught in programming class to solve other types of problems. For example, they talk about systematically testing and debugging a broken bicycle, or about dividing a difficult assignment into simpler subparts. Programming also leads students to appreciate the need for careful, precise work. Ms. Byron said that, for example, some children have become much more careful about punctuation and grammar in their writing after they learned to check all the details in their programs.

Many students enjoy creating their own programs. In fact, for some students, programming is one of their favorite activities both at school and at home. One sixth-grade student said "It's almost like magic to make the computer do what you want." This reminded Ms. Byron of a description of the joys of programming she had read recently:

> The programmer, like the poet, works only slightly removed from pure thought-stuff.... Few media of creation are so flexible, so easy to polish and rework, so readily capable of realizing grand conceptual structures.
>
> Yet the program construct, unlike the poet's words, is real in the sense that it moves and works, producing visible outputs separate from the construct itself. It prints results, draws pictures, produces sounds, moves arms. The magic of myth and legend has come true in our time. One types

the correct incantation on a keyboard, and a display screen comes to life, showing things that never were nor could be.*

WHICH PROGRAMMING LANGUAGE SHOULD BE TAUGHT?

While everyone at Babbage School agrees students should learn to program, there is a debate about whether BASIC or Logo is the best language for them to learn. This same debate is occurring in many other schools. The principal at Babbage School appointed a committee to compare the two languages and provide guidelines for the other teachers. The committee consisted of two teachers who are knowledgeable about programming, two teachers who are novice programmers, and two students from the computer club.

The committee members began by discussing what criteria they should use to decide which language is better for teaching children. After discussing the matter with other teachers and students, they agreed upon the following four criteria:

1. It should be easy to get started with the language, so children can quickly begin to write, test and debug simple programs. This is important for motivating students and alleviating anxieties about programming.

2. The language should be compatible with the way children think. It should contain commands for working with pictures and words that are easy for children to understand.

3. Working with the language should encourage students to develop good problem solving and programming techniques. It should provide a solid basis for learning other computer languages and mastering sophisticated programming techniques.

4. The language should be readily available for the various models of personal computers, including inexpensive ones. This is important because many students want to learn to program computers they have at home.

The members of the programming language committee found this set of criteria helped them organize and describe the characteristics of BASIC and Logo. They also found that there are different versions of each language, and some versions have significant

* Frederick P. Brooks, *The Mythical Man-Month* (Reading, MA: Addison-Wesley, 1974) pp.7-8.

advantages over others. For example, some versions of BASIC have commands that make it easy to create pictures, while others do not. Some versions of Logo contain turtle graphics commands only and lack commands for working with words. Others have a full set of list processing commands for working with words. The committee decided to compare the most complete versions of BASIC and Logo available for the personal computers used in the school.

On the first criterion, ease of getting started with small programs, the committee gave high ratings to both BASIC and Logo. Both languages let students easily enter programs, immediately run and check them, and, if necessary, make corrections. Both also allow students to stop a program at any point and check the values of variables, and even to make the program run slowly so they can watch what happens at each step.

Logo has definite advantages on the second criterion, compatibility with children's ways of thinking and understanding. Children are best able to understand things in terms of concrete images and their own actions. Turtle graphics therefore provides an excellent means of introducing children to programming. Commands to the turtle reflect processes children can act out. For example, a child might begin creating a SQUARE procedure by drawing a square on paper or walking the shape of a square. The child can observe his own movements and then tell the turtle how to follow the same pattern. In contrast, the usual graphics commands in BASIC require an understanding of X-Y coordinates and do not reflect the processes of drawing or moving.

The overall structure of Logo is also better suited to children than the overall structure in BASIC. With Logo, children can think of procedures in terms of teaching the computer new words. Once the computer is taught a procedure, it can be instructed to do it just by typing the procedure's name. With BASIC, children have to keep track of the numbers of lines that contain the commands for each function, and they have to be careful about how these commands interact with other parts of the program.

The third criterion is that the language should encourage good problem solving and programming techniques. Both BASIC and Logo can do this to some extent. However, Logo has some important advantages on this criterion.

The committee emphasized the importance of teaching students the techniques of *structured* or *modular* programming. Structured programming emphasizes that programmers should carefully analyze the task the program is to perform and divide it into simpler subgoals. Each subgoal should then be handled in its own section or *module* of the program. Modules should be coded, tested and debugged independently, and then combined into the complete program. Carefully designing the program and working with modules makes the coding, testing and debugging stages easier. Structured programs are more likely to work correctly, and are easier to revise and extend than programs that do not have a modular structure.

Another aspect of structured programming is that the program should be easy for people to read and understand. Dividing the program into modules and giving each module and variable a name describing its function helps make the program readable.

The use of procedures in Logo encourages structured programming. Once a procedure is developed and tested, it can be easily combined with other procedures. You can even use the same variable name in two different procedures, and the computer will keep track of them separately. (This is not the case with BASIC.) With Logo, you can also give procedures and variables long names that describe their functions. BASIC does not encourage these aspects of structured programming.

BASIC has clear advantages on the final criterion, availability for many different personal computers. BASIC is the standard language that comes with most personal computers, including the least expensive ones. Logo requires a more powerful computer system than BASIC, and so is not as widely available.

After viewing how the languages fit the criteria, the committee recommended that Logo be used as the first language taught in the introductory class. However, they also recommended that some BASIC be taught at the end of the course, especially for students who have computers with BASIC at home.

The committee also discussed another language, called Pascal. Pascal is a powerful, well structured language that contains many sophisticated programming constructs. It is excellent for encouraging good problem solving and programming techniques, and for writing large, sophisticated programs. However, students find it much more difficult to get started with Pascal than with Logo or BASIC. Also, Pascal is not widely available for inexpensive personal computers. The committee recommended that Pascal be available in an optional advanced course for interested students who have already become proficient in Logo or BASIC.

The committee's final guidelines emphasized that students can learn a great deal while working with any programming language. The members stated their most important guideline is that students be encouraged to systematically analyze the tasks their programs are to perform; follow the principles of structured programming; and carefully attend to the details of program coding, testing, and debugging.

Chapter 10

Computer Aids for the Physically Handicapped

Impaired vision, hearing, speech or movement limits many people's abilities to communicate, learn, work and control their environment. Personal computers, combined with special devices and programs, can lessen the impact of these impairments. Computers make it possible for handicapped individuals to better substitute intact abilities for impaired ones; receive more effective special training; use information that is otherwise inaccessible to them; and enjoy new opportunities for education, employment, social interactions and recreation.

Blind people can use computers with devices and programs for producing speech. With a *speech synthesizer,* any word that appears on the screen can be pronounced by the computer. This gives blind people access to most of the computer's capabilities. In addition, *pattern recognition* devices and programs, combined with special output devices, make it possible for computers to translate written words into tactile patterns, braille or speech. These systems allow blind people to use any book, magazine or newspaper without being dependent upon others to read to them.

People with vocal impairments can also use computer-synthesized speech. By typing messages on the keyboard for the computer to pronounce, a mute person can communicate via a telephone or with a person who cannot read. In addition, computerized message systems provide a means of rapid, long-distance communication that is especially valuable for people whose speech or hearing impairments prohibit them from using standard telephones.

Computers are also valuable aids for people with motor impairments. Information systems bring large data bases to people who cannot go to a library. Computer-controlled actuators (e.g., robot arms) can be programmed to perform patterns of movements and sense when they come into contact with an object. These provide motorically handicapped persons with a way of manipulating objects to perform such functions as eating, turning the pages of books and changing the disks in their computer's disk drive.

Many people lack adequate manual dexterity to use a standard computer keyboard, but are able to move their arms and hands. Special keyboards with large, touch sensitive keys make it possible for these people to use all the capabilities of computers. For other people who cannot use any sort of keyboard, *speech recognition* devices let them use their voice to operate the computer. In addition, special input devices have been developed for people who have both severe vocal and motor handicaps, so they can use computers as communication aids and for other purposes.

Computers are also useful in teaching handicapped individuals. The capability of computers to individualize lessons by adjusting the level of difficulty, amount of repetition and speed of presentation of the material can be especially valuable for many handicapped students. For example, computers can be programmed to be "infinitely patient" with students whose handicaps cause them to respond very slowly or require many repetitions. In addition, computers help provide special training to compensate for impairments. For example, a computer with a special sound analysis device can help deaf people learn to pronounce words by providing visual cues comparing how a word should sound and how the individual just pronounced it. This type of "cross-modality" feedback can help a deaf person compensate, at least in part, for the inability to hear and compare the sounds.

With computerized aids such as those described in this chapter, many handicapped children can be educated in a school such as Babbage. Computerized aids can also help severely handicapped children who require more special care and teaching than is feasible within a standard school. The next section describes the development of a communication aid for one severely handicapped person.

DEVELOPING A COMMUNICATION AID

Jane has cerebral palsy and has always been confined to a wheel chair. She can move her arms but has poor control of them, so every movement requires time and effort. Her vocalizations are limited to a few grunts and clicks, which she uses to communicate *yes* and *no*. Jane understands everything said to her and has learned to read fairly well. Her difficulties in communicating are due to her physical inability to produce language in any form—spoken, written or sign—not due to a lack of knowledge or intelligence. Jane's experiences provide a good example of how computers can be used to improve the life of handicapped people, and of how such work has been progressing at some research and education centers.

For most of her life, Jane has used communication boards. These boards have 100 or more squares, each containing a letter, number, word or phrase. The board sits on Jane's lap and she communicates by pointing to the squares on it. This is slow and physically difficult for Jane, and it is tedious for the receiver of the message who has to watch as Jane points to each square. Since it takes Jane several minutes of tiring work for even a simple message, and the other person must be watching the entire time, her communications with the board have been limited almost entirely to her immediate needs.

Jane lives at a center for physically handicapped people, and several of the workers there have been developing computerized aids to help her. There is little money available for the work they are doing, and the workers have volunteered their time and expertise.

Jane's aids are based upon a standard personal computer system that costs about $400, combined with a special input device and programs her friends have developed. The use of a standard personal computer provides more flexibility and is less expensive than systems built specifically for handicapped people. However, since the needed input devices and programs are not yet available for most personal computers, Jane's friends had to develop their own. They have already created, tested and revised several programs.

Special Hardware

Jane's friends have created a special switch and connected it to the computer. The switch is held in a headband. It closes whenever Jane tilts her head to the left and opens whenever she holds her head upright or moves it to the right. This switch takes advantage of the muscles Jane controls most easily. She finds the head movements much easier than the arm movements necessary to point to the communication board.

Jane's friends found an easy and inexpensive way to interface her head switch to the computer. The computer, like many personal computers, has a built-in connector for plugging in the joysticks used in many games. Jane's head switch plugs into the computer in place of a joystick. Closing the head switch sends the same signal to the computer as pressing the button on a joystick. It is therefore easy to write programs that check when the switch is closed.

Special Software

The next step was to program the computer so Jane could use it in place of the communication board. The first program was very simple, but still offered important advantages over the communication board. The program displayed the letters of the alphabet; a period, comma and question mark; and boxes for a space, for erasing, and for sounding a bell. An arrow moves over the characters on the screen. The arrow is called a *scanner*, since it scans over the items displayed. Jane selects a character by closing her head switch when the scanner is directly above the desired one. As she selects each character, it is added to the message area at the top of the screen. When the message is complete, she selects the bell and the computer sounds a tone to let people know that a message is ready. Figure 10.1 shows the screen as Jane is creating a message.

FIGURE 10.1   A simple scanning system. The scanner is above the letter O.

This system, which can be set up fairly easily with most personal computers, significantly improved Jane's communication possibilities. Although communicating with it is still much slower than speaking, Jane can form messages more quickly and easily than ever before. Since the message remains on the screen until erased, and Jane sounds the bell when it is complete, the other person does not have to be present and watching while it is created. Also, the written messages are less often misunderstood than when the communication board was used. These improvements led Jane to communicate much more than she had previously.

The initial scanning program has been improved several times. As Jane became accustomed to it, she could accurately select the letters more rapidly. Since the speed of the scanner was set in the program, it was easily adjusted. Jane's friends have experimented with different speeds to determine the fastest one with which she is comfortable.

Jane's friends have also tested different arrangements of the letters on the screen. In one program, the letters were arranged by frequency of use. Each time a letter is selected, the scanner returns to the first, most often used, letter. This decreases the average time Jane must wait for the scanner to reach the letter she wants to select.

A more sophisticated program uses two-way scanner movement to increase Jane's communication speed even more. First the scanner moves vertically and Jane selects the row containing the letter she wants. Then the scanner moves horizontally and Jane selects the particular letter. Figure 10.2 shows an example. The next letter Jane wants to select is a G. She waits until the arrow scanner points to the row with G, and then uses her switch. The scanner then changes to an arrow pointing down that moves over the letters in the row. Jane uses her switch again when it points to the G. The letters are arranged so those used most frequently can be selected most rapidly, and numbers have also been added. This system minimizes the average time Jane must wait for the scanner to reach a letter.

Jane has become very efficient at using the row and column scanner system. A more recent program has further improved the system by adding frequently used words. Since the screen does not have enough space for all the needed words at one time, the program was designed so Jane can cause different sets of words to appear. For example, one set contains words relevant to eating, another set contains names of places and people. The bottom row of each screen display contains special squares. Jane can select which

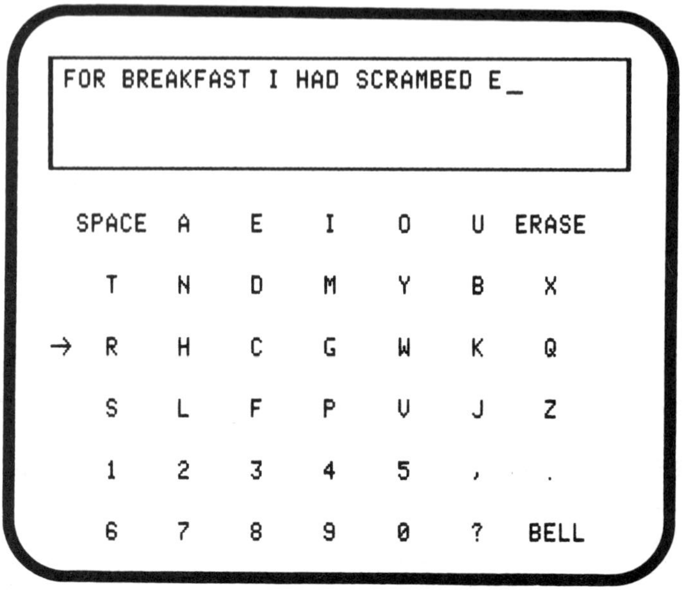

FIGURE 10.2   A row/column scanning system, organized so the most frequently used letters can be selected most quickly.

set of words appears on the screen by using her head-switch when the scanner is on the appropriate box. Jane can combine words from the different sets to form a message. With this technique of changing what is on the screen, many words and phrases can be added to Jane's message program.

More recently, a printer has been added to the system. Selecting one of the special squares causes the computer to print the message. This makes it possible for Jane to create longer messages and to write letters. She can communicate much more rapidly and effectively then ever before, and has begun to start conversations and ask many more questions. Soon, her friends will add a speech synthesizer to the system, so Jane can communicate with people who cannot read her messages.

Limitations of Jane's System

These computerized aids have vastly improved Jane's communication possibilities and significantly improved her life. However there are two critical limitations that her friends would like to remedy.

One limitation is that Jane cannot use most available computer programs with her special input system. Each program must be revised to accept inputs from the head switch before she can use it. For a few programs, the necessary revisions are fairly simple, and one of Jane's friends has revised some computer games and lessons for her. However, for most programs it is extremely difficult to make the neccesary modifications.

The remedy to this limitation is to create a special input system that can replace the standard computer keyboard and that sends the same signals to the computer as the standard keyboard. This type of input system is called a *keyboard emulator*. Since a letter or number entered with a keyboard emulator sends the same signal to the computer as a standard keyboard, the emulator can replace the keyboard and programs do not have to be modified.

Unfortunately, a scanning system that functions as a keyboard emulator is more complex to build than the systems Jane's friends have created so far. They are experimenting with using an inexpensive computer (which costs less than $100) to control the scanning system. This small computer would then send the appropriate signals to a second, larger computer that actually runs the programs Jane wants to use. When they succeed, Jane will have complete access to all the capabilities of the computer. She will be able to use educational programs, write with word processing programs, create computer music and pictures, access information, send and receive messages via communication networks, play computer games and learn to program. Jane has told her friends that when they build a keyboard emulator she will take care of entering names and addresses into the center's computerized mailing list and she will learn to write programs for them. This will be Jane's first opportunity for useful work.

The other serious limitation of Jane's system is that it is not portable. When she is away from it, she has to resort to the communication board. Jane hopes to be able to obtain a special portable communication device, called the *Express 3*, which has its own built-in computer and can function similarly to the latest program her friends have designed. However, it is expensive and, since it is a specialized communication device, it does not provide access to all the other capabilities of a computer.

Jane's experiences illustrate the potential of computers to help individuals with severe physical handicaps. A number of people are now using scanning systems similar to Jane's, each individualized with appropriate switches, scanning rates, and sets of words.

The development of computer aids for the handicapped is an exciting area of current research. The remainder of this chapter describes special input devices, output devices and programs that can serve people with impaired vision, hearing, speech or movement.

LARGE CHARACTER DISPLAYS AND PRINTOUTS

Many people with partially impaired vision cannot read normal print but can read large, high-contrast print. There are two ways to create large letters on computer screens. One is to simply use a television or video monitor with a large display screen. The other is to use the computer's graphics capability to create large letters. In addition, many computer printers can produce large type on paper. With a suitable printer, any information stored in the computer can be printed in large letters.

COMPUTER GENERATED SPEECH

Many people are unable to see any print, no matter how large. Computer generated speech can be especially valuable for them. There are two general types of computer generated speech: *stored vocabulary* and *unlimited vocabulary*.

When stored vocabulary speech is used, sound patterns of a person saying the words are stored in the computer's memory. Special devices and programs measure characteristics of the sound waveform as the person pronounces each word. Numbers representing the waveform at each fraction of a second are stored in the computer. That is, the speech waveform (an example of what is technically called *analog* information) is converted to a sequence of numbers (technically called *digital* information). The numbers are then used to recreate the sound of the word whenever it is needed.

Stored vocabulary speech can sound very human when individual words are produced, but it usually sounds somewhat unnatural when the words are combined into sentences. With this technique, the computer is limited to the words previously stored in its memory. Each digitized word requires a large amount of memory—many numbers must be stored for the computer to recreate the spoken word clearly—so the vocabulary of a personal computer with digitized speech is limited. However, the possibilities for digitized speech will expand as larger capacity computer memories become less expensive and as more efficient techniques are developed for representing speech waveforms within the computer's memory.

With unlimited vocabulary speech, programs for generating the individual speech sounds (phonemes) are stored in the computer, along with rules for combining them into words, phrases and sentences. This technique of *speech synthesis* enables the computer to produce any word from its component sounds. Synthesized speech typically does not sound as natural as digitized speech, but it has been improved greatly in recent years. Some systems now even approximate human intonation patterns when words are combined into sentences.

Phoneme synthesis techniques have been combined with *text-to-speech conversion* programs. These programs contain a set of rules that tell the computer how to change any sequence of letters into speech. Creating a program of this sort for English is difficult, since no one has found the perfect set of rules for converting written words to speech. Many letters and letter patterns are pronounced in various ways depending on the context of their use. For example, the word *read* is pronounced differently depending on whether it is referring to the past or future (e.g., "John read the book" versus "John will read the book"). The same aspects of English that cause difficulties for people in learning to read also cause difficulties in programming computers to convert written English to spoken English.

Despite the limitations, phoneme synthesis and text-to-speech programs are extremely valuable for blind people and others who cannot read. After a short time getting used to the computer's speech, people find it easy to understand. Most people report it is like adapting to someone who has a foreign accent and mispronounces some words.

CONVERTING LETTERS TO TACTILE FORMS

Print can also be made accessible to blind people by converting it to tactile form. One device, already used by many blind people, converts printed letters and symbols to an enlarged vibrating form. This device, called the *Optacon*, consists of a small camera, an electronics unit and a stimulator array. The array is composed of 144 miniature rods. The electronics unit interprets the light pattern received by the camera and sends signals that cause certain rods to vibrate, thereby producing a tactile analogue to the light pattern. Some training is necessary to learn to read the vibrating patterns, but once this is mastered the blind person has access to all printed materials. Special adaptors are available so the Optacon can be used to read computer screen and calculator displays.

Other devices use braille. Braille is a system of writing in which each letter is represented by a pattern of raised dots in a 2 by 3 grid. Blind people read by feeling the dot patterns. Although widely used, braille has several disadvantages. Braille books are extremely bulky: A standard student dictionary fills a box three feet on each side. Braille typewriters are noisy and slow. Braille type cannot be corrected, since the raised dots cannot be erased. Braille books are therefore expensive, and most books, newspapers and magazines are never made available in braille (or any other medium, such as tape recordings, accessible to blind people).

Special braille printers can be interfaced to computers so any information in the computer can be transformed to braille easily. This provides a remedy for the problem of braille not being correctable. A word processing program can be used and, after all corrections are made on the computer screen, a braille copy produced.

Other braille output devices can also be interfaced to computers. One example is a device that contains sets of pins arranged in the 2 by 3 braille grid. Each pin can be raised or lowered, thereby providing a mechanical braille display. This device can be controlled by computer programs to produce instant braille for a blind computer user. Information stored in the computer can be transformed to braille as it is being read.

A special device called a *VersaBraille*™ contains a mechanical braille display, a cassette information storage component and a specially designed braille keyboard, all under the control of a built-in computer. Information can be entered from the keyboard, corrected (editing capabilities are built-in), stored on cassette and transformed to braille whenever needed. The VersaBraille provides a solution to the bulkiness of braille. It is easily carried, and 400 pages of braille can be stored on a standard cassette tape. In addition, the VersaBraille can be interfaced to computers so information can be transferred between the computer and the cassette storage system within the VersaBraille. A blind person can transfer information from the computer to the VersaBraille and then read it where and when it is convenient. Information entered into the VersaBraille can be transferred to the computer to be printed, stored, or sent to others via a communication network.

COMPUTERIZED LETTER RECOGNITION AND AUTOMATIC READING MACHINES

Speech synthesizers and text-to-speech programs can convert any words stored in a computer to speech. Other devices can convert information stored in a computer to large letter displays or to braille. However, much of the information handicapped people need is in books, not computers. To fully use the capability of computers to convert text to speech, braille or large print, we need an efficient way of transferring text from books to computers' memories.

Special cameras and *pattern recognition* programs have been used for some time to recognize specially designed letters and numbers, such as those used for account numbers on checks. The camera converts the pattern of each letter into a binary code. A computer can be programmed to process the binary code and determine which letter it represents. In the last few years, devices and programs have been developed to make computers able to recognize most typewritten characters and adjust automatically for different type fonts and sizes. Current devices work well with typewritten words, and more reliable and less expensive devices will become available in the next few years. Unfortunately, only very limited success has been obtained with handwritten letters, due to the large variations found even within one person's handwriting.

Letter recognition devices can be combined with special output devices, such as those that produce large size displays, speech or braille. Letter recognition devices can also be combined with braille printers to expedite the production of braille books.

One impressive example of technology to serve the handicapped is the *Kurzweil Reading Machine,* which converts print to speech for the blind. This machine combines sophisticated pattern recognition, speech synthesis, and text-to-speech conversion capabilities. It lets the blind users control how the material is read. They can set the speed of reading and adjust the tonality of the voice. They can stop the reading at any time, have the last few words or lines repeated, request the machine to spell out words or announce punctuation and capitalization, and mark certain words or phrases for later reference. Unfortunately, this reading machine is a very expensive device.

SPECIAL KEYBOARDS

Many people lack the hand dexterity and control to use standard keyboards, but are not limited to single switch input devices such as the one described earlier in this chapter. Special keyboards have been designed to enable these people to use computers. These keyboards can replace the standard one on most personal computers. Since the special keyboards send the exact same signals to the computer as standard ones, all software can be used without modification.

Some special keyboards simply have large keys, so less exact control is required to use them. Others also have touch sensitive keys, so that the key only has to be touched, not pressed. People who cannot use their arms can use these keyboards with mouth sticks or pointers attached to headbands.

Some people have trouble directing their hand pointer to the appropriate key even with a large keyboard, but once they reach the right key they can keep touching it easily. These people typically make many typing errors because they hit inappropriate keys while moving toward the desired one. One solution to this problem is to set the keyboard so that a key must be touched for a certain period of time before it sends a signal to the computer. The optimal time for minimizing errors but maximizing typing speed can be found for each individual. In addition, the keyboard can be rearranged so the most frequently used keys are located where the individual is able to reach them most easily.

SPEECH RECOGNITION BY COMPUTERS

Some people cannot use any type of keyboard but can speak. Speech input devices make computers accessible to them.

A great deal of research has been devoted to getting computers to recognize people's speech. This research has shown that speech is very complex and we do not fully understand how people are able to recognize spoken words so easily. It is much more difficult to make computers recognize spoken words than it is to make them pronounce words. However, advances have been made and some usable, although limited, devices are now available. This is another area in which great progress is expected in the next few years.

Currently available systems require the user to "train" the computer to distinguish among a number of spoken words. The technique is related to the computer-generated, stored vocabulary speech previously discussed. The individual selects a vocabulary to be used and pronounces each word. The computer digitizes the sound patterns and stores a set of numbers representing the waveform of the word. Once trained, the computer recognizes a spoken word by digitizing it and comparing the resulting pattern of numbers to the patterns already stored in its memory. Since each time an individual says a word the pronounciation changes slightly, exact matches are not expected, but the computer is programmed to find the closest match. Since people differ widely in their speech patterns, these systems are reliable only in recognizing the words spoken by the person who said the original training set.

The digitized representation of each word takes a lot of memory, and the matching process becomes progressively slower and less reliable as more words are added. Therefore, speech recognition systems work well only with limited vocabularies. Currently available systems typically handle fewer than 100 words at a time. Although limited, this is a sufficient number of words for many purposes. For example, some speech recognition devices can function as keyboard emulators. The vocabulary used would consist of the labels for the keys. This lets people use all standard programs by saying the labels of keys rather than pressing them.

CONCLUSION

I have described some of the existing types of devices and programs that can aid handicapped individuals. Other systems now available or being developed and tested include: flexible and portable communication devices for people who cannot speak; portable terminals to let deaf people send and receive messages from any telephone; environmental control systems that let physically disabled people control lights, televisions and other devices from the computer; computer controlled robots; and input systems that check where a person's eyes are focused, so one can select among options displayed on the screen simply by focusing on the desired choice for a few seconds.

Versions of all these computerized aids exist now, but in many cases they are very expensive and not widely available. I expect that within the next few years more powerful, reliable, portable and affordable versions of these systems will become available, and that new and powerful aids for handicapped people will be created.

The available technology strongly influences our concepts of what constitutes a handicap. For example, many people with poor vision or hearing function perfectly well only because eyeglasses and hearing aids compensate for their impairments. As computerized aids for the handicapped are further developed and made widely available, other physical impairments may come to be considered minor inconveniences rather than severe handicaps.

Chapter 11

Toward Babbage School

Learning—gaining knowledge, understanding or skill—can be accomplished in many ways. We learn by listening to teachers' presentations, reading books and viewing films. We learn by exploring new objects, situations and places, and we learn by practicing skills. We learn when we create a story, picture or song. We learn when we build a model or solve a puzzle. We learn when we communicate and when we play.

The aim of this book has been to convey the diverse ways personal computers can contribute to teaching and learning. Through examples and discussion, I have portrayed some of the wide variety of topics, students, teaching methods, and situations computers can serve. Computers can aid in the teaching of every subject, from sciences to the humanities, from mathematics to foreign languages. They can help make traditional means of teaching more effective, and they can open new approaches to teaching and learning. They can help students master basic reading, writing and arithmetic skills, as well as encourage the development of thinking, problem solving, and research skills. They can be used by very young children, students with learning difficulties, and the most advanced and gifted students. They can be used by individuals and by groups. In addition to being educational tools, computers are themselves a topic about which students need to learn.

I have presented the potential of computers within the context of an idealized school called Babbage. While Babbage School is

171

fictional, every use of computers I have described is feasible right now and, in fact, is already taking place at some schools, homes, research sites, or special education centers. Computers are also being used as educational tools in businesses, museums, libraries, science centers and summer camps.

I have limited the examples in this book to the capabilities of computers that are already widely used in schools and homes. However, computer technology continues to develop rapidly. New computers and peripherals provide more internal memory, larger capacity external memories with faster rates of information transfer, higher resolution and more colorful graphics, faster and more sophisticated animations, improved speech production and recognition capabilities, and much, much more. As the technology advances, the cost of computer systems is decreasing dramatically. Educational software is also improving rapidly, as developers learn to take better advantage of the potential of computers and begin to create educational programs for more powerful machines. As we gain experience and the technology advances, we will continue to discover educational uses for computers. We have only begun to realize the potential of this new technology.

LEARNING MORE ABOUT COMPUTERS

If you are interested in using computers as educational tools, this book is just the beginning step. Learning more about computers requires experiential learning. The next step is to buy, rent or borrow a computer, and start working with it. Computers are becoming more readily available. If your school does not have one you can use, perhaps a local dealer rents machines, or your library may have one available. Stores that rent time on computers have opened in many cities.

Once you have access to a computer, try all the software you can find. Perhaps your school office has a word processing program, or Visicalc®, or a filing program. Try to find some lesson, drill, game and simulation programs, as well as graphics creation and music composition tools. They won't all be great programs—some of them will probably be terrible. But trying them will give you a much better idea of what computers can do. Think about the programs you try, how they can be improved and expanded, made more flexible or easier to use. Ask others about their favorite program, what it does and why they like it. Particularly ask children, and find out whether they like to use computers and why. Observe children as they use computers. Find out whether there is a local users club and whether they have a public-domain software library. Try writing your own simple program in BASIC or, if it is available, Logo. If you are not ready to write your own program, try to figure out and modify a program someone else has written, or get some of the books and magazines with program listings (see Appendix B) and enter one into the computer. Experiment, explore, observe, criticize, create—and learn about the potential of computers as educational tools.

GETTING STARTED USING COMPUTERS IN SCHOOLS

We have seen that computers can be valuable additions to the textbooks, chalk boards, films and other tools already common in schools. Like these other tools, the value of computers depends completely upon how well we use them. When we choose a book for students, we consider whether it contains appropriate material, how well it is written and at what level, whether it will interest students, how it will fit with other materials, and so on. Similar decisions must be made about each computer program. The success of computers as educational tools depends completely upon the quality and appropriateness of the software selected, and the manner in which computers are integrated with other educational activities.

In many schools, individual teachers, parents or students have brought computers into classrooms. Since the person who does so is typically knowledgeable and excited about computers, these individual innovators are usually successful in teaching children with computers and about them. However, implementing computers on a school-wide or district-wide basis is a more complex task, one that requires a great deal of thought, careful planning and ongoing effort. In this section, I briefly discuss some of the practical issues and concerns that must addressed when using computers as educational tools. Appendix B lists sources of more detailed information about the processes, decisions, joys and difficulties involved.

Computer Awareness

The first step towards using computers as educational tools is for teachers, administrators, parents and students to become aware of the possibilities and interested in trying some of them. Understanding the possible uses of computers and having a general understanding of their nature is often called *computer awareness*. Reading this book should be sufficient for gaining a fair level of computer awareness.

Computer Comfort

The next step is *computer comfort*. This requires actually using a computer and becoming comfortable with the mechanics of loading and running programs, entering information, using printers and so on. There is no substitute for "hands-on" experience with a computer for coming to appreciate its potential. At this stage, it is best to try a variety of programs to experience the different possibilities. The aim is to develop more concrete knowledge about what computers can do, as well as critical skills in evaluating software.

Making Decisions About Computers

Once past the awareness and comfort levels, the real work begins. Decisions have to be made about how computers will be used and whether some students or classes will have priority over others. How will computers be integrated into the curriculum at each grade level? Will they be used primarily for lessons and drills or to teach computer programming? If programming is to be taught, which language will be selected? Should the computers be used primarily in math and science classes or mainly for word processing? Will educational computer games be used? What about computer art and music? Will all students get equal access to the computers? Should gifted children or those in need of remedial assistance be given priority? Will the computers be placed in classrooms, the library or a special computer laboratory room? How will their use be supervised, and who will do so? Who can take care of maintenance and showing others how to properly use the computers?

After decisions are made about how the computers will be used, by whom, and in what settings, it is time to start selecting hardware and software. Again, there are many questions. Should one brand of computers be purchased, or are different ones best for different purposes? For which brands of computers is the best software available? For which computers are good versions of the BASIC, Logo and Pascal languages available? How much internal memory is needed, and are disk drives and printers needed for each computer? Are color video monitors essential, or will black-and-white do? Are modems needed? Which word processing program is best for students? What about lesson and drill programs? Where can good science simulations be obtained? These are just some of the questions that may need to be addressed. Which questions are most important, and the appropriate answers to each, depends upon the prior decisions about how computers will be used, as well as the constraints imposed by the available budget, space and personal.

At this stage, careful budget planning is critical so that sufficient money will be available for software, needed peripherals (such a printers), staff training, maintenance and supplies (such as disks and paper). This point cannot be overemphasized. Many schools have invested all their available funds in hardware, only to discover that it is useless without appropriate software and staff training.

Once the computers are installed, there is another set of concerns. How will new requests to use computers be handled? What about keeping up with new developments and the on-going acquisition of new hardware and software? What should be done to encourage students and teachers who are uncomfortable using computers? What should be done about students who are so interested in computers they neglect others areas of study? How are computers changing the social structure of classes? Has a group of interested students evolved into a "computer elite" who try to monopolize the computers? If so, how can they be led to serve as "peer tutors" who will help and encourage the other students? Will teachers be uncomfortable because some students will know more than they do about the computers? What about students interested in more advanced programming or in forming a computer club?

As with any educational innovation, many new issues and questions will arise. These issues and questions present an exciting new challenge to educators—the challenge to adapt new technology to improve children's education.

THE LIMITATIONS OF COMPUTERS

While computers can serve many valuable educational functions, they can not solve all the problems of education. They do not help us decide what to teach or how to teach it. Computers can be used whether we choose to emphasize basic reading, writing and arithmetic skills; rote memory of facts; or thinking skills. They can be used in the most competitive settings and the most cooperative ones, in the most structured classrooms and the most open ones. They can be used in conjunction with the best teaching practices and with the worst. Depending upon how we use them, computers can bore or motivate, intimidate or encourage, threaten or challenge.

The introduction of computers does not solve the issues of equal opportunity in schools. In fact, it brings these issues into the limelight. Will computers be introduced in a way that will encourage boys to learn programming but discourage girls? Will computers be available in the inner-city schools as well as the suburban schools? Will computers be used to direct remedial students in drills while they are used to encourage creativity and problem solving for others? That is, will some children learn to be directed by computers while others will learn how to direct computers?

Computers are tools, not decision makers. No matter how powerful computers become, they can never resolve the difficult, classical issues of education—what we choose to emphasize in schools, what teaching methods we employ, how we organize our schools and our classrooms, what standards we set for students, and how we can best distribute the limited resources available for education.

THE ROAD TO BABBAGE SCHOOL

Babbage School—an idealized school of the future—is an attractive place. While the necessary technology already exists, Babbage School is far away from current schools. Only part of the road to Babbage School has been paved and mapped; the remainder is rocky and potholed, with many unknown twists and turns. There are some beautiful vistas along the way, where we can observe children gaining new insights and skills. But we are also likely to take some wrong turns and experience difficulties and frustrations. And we will encounter people who tell us that the journey is not worthwhile, or that we have gone far enough when we have only begun. Why proceed down the road toward Babbage School? Because it is the road to schools that will prepare the children of today for the world in which they will live.

Appendix A

The Inner Workings of a Computer

In this appendix, I describe how information is represented and processed within a computer. The discussion is at a conceptual, non-technical level. While you do not have to know about the computer's inner workings in order to use one, the information in this appendix will help you gain more insight into the potential and limitations of computers. It will also provide a good base of knowledge for learning more about computers.

HOW INFORMATION IS REPRESENTED IN COMPUTERS

At their most fundamental level of operation, computers distinguish between only two different symbols, which are referred to as 0 and 1. This is a convenient and reliable system: It is easy to code the 0s and 1s inside the computer as two electrical states, such as on and off or high and low voltage. All information in the computer is represented by sequences of these two symbols. That is, computers use a *binary* (two-part) system. Each 0 or 1 is called a *bit*, a shortened form of *binary digit*. Many computers operate on groups of eight bits at a time, so a group of eight bits is given a special name: *byte*. Computers use binary representations—sequences of bits—to store and process numbers, words, pictures and sounds.

Representing Numbers

In the familiar decimal system, numbers are represented by the digits 0, 1, 2, 3, 4, 5, 6, 7, 8 and 9. These ten digits can be combined to form any integer. Your height and the distance from the earth to the sun, your salary and the federal budget can be represented equally well.

How can computers represent the digits zero through nine when all they have to work with are the 0s and 1s of the binary system? The digits zero and one are easy, being represented in binary by 0 and 1. But what about two? Since we have already used both available symbols, we must combine symbols: Two is represented in binary by 10. This looks like ten in the decimal system, and there is a relationship. The decimal system has ten different symbols, and so it can represent ten numbers (zero through nine) with one symbol each. For the eleventh number, two symbols must be combined. Since in the binary system there are only two different symbols, symbols must be combined to represent the third number.

Table A.1 gives the binary equivalents for the decimal numbers one to ten and for some larger numbers. This table shows that the largest decimal number that can be represented with one byte (eight bits) is 255 and the largest number that can be represented with two bytes (sixteen bits) is 65,535. Examining Table A.1 reveals some patterns that suggest mathematical operations can be performed upon binary numbers. For example, to multiply a number by two in the binary system, you simply place a zero to the right of the number. (Notice the parallel to multiplying by ten in the decimal system.) Computers use binary arithmetic for all calculations.

Representing Letters and Words

The binary system is an effective way for computers to represent numbers. But what about language rather than math? In English, there are 26 lower-case letters and 26 upper-case letters. There are also punctuation symbols, such as the period, comma, colon, and apostrophe, and other frequently used symbols, such as the dollar sign and percent symbol. All these language symbols are represented in computers by sequences of 0s and 1s.

Each language symbol is typically represented by a sequence of eight bits or one byte. With eight bits, it is possible to represent 256 different items (2 to the 8th power). This provides enough different sequences for all the necessary language symbols, with many left over to represent special things for the computer (these

TABLE A.1
The Binary Equivalents for Some Decimal Numbers

Decimal Number	Binary Numbers
O	0
1	1
2	10
3	11
4	100
5	101
6	110
7	111
8	1000
9	1001
10	1010
20	10100
30	11110
40	101000
50	110010
100	1100100
200	11001000
255	11111111
1000	1111101000
65535	1111111111111111

differ depending on the computer). Most personal computers follow a standard known as the American Standard Code for Information Interchange or ASCII. The ASCII codes for some letters and other symbols are shown in Table A.2.

Representing Pictures

A computer screen consists of a grid of many dots of light, each of which can be either on or off. A picture is created by turning certain dots of light on. Consider, for example, how simple line drawings of smiling and frowning faces might be represented. Suppose we had 144 light bulbs arranged in a 12 by 12 grid. By turning on different patterns of bulbs, we could create images of smiling and frowning faces, as shown in Figure A.1.

These pictures are very simple, but with many small dots of light we could create much more detailed images. Although a good

TABLE A.2
ASCII Codes for Some Language Symbols

Language Symbol	ASCII Code
A	01000001
a	01100001
B	01000010
b	01100010
C	01000011
c	01100011
M	01001101
m	01101101
Z	01001010
z	01101010
"	00100010
$	00100100
.	00101110
,	00101100

quality picture will require a large number of dots of light, each one is either on or off—a binary choice. Using 1 for on and 0 for off, the grid can be represented by a sequence of bits. For example, the top line of the smiling face would be represented by the binary string 001111111100.

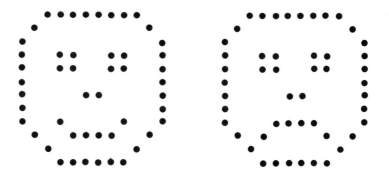

FIGURE A.1 Smiling and frowning faces, each created by dots in a 12 by 12 grid.

The same general idea can be extended to represent color pictures. On some computer systems, each dot on the screen can be any of four colors. Each dot must then be represented by two bits, allowing the computer to distinguish among four possibilities.

You may have noticed that a given string of bits can represent a number, a language symbol, or a picture. For example, the ASCII code for the letter A also represents the decimal number 65, and the top line of the smiling face is represented by the same sequence of bits as the decimal number 1020. The computer has to keep track of when to treat sequences of bits as numbers, letters or pictures. When a binary code is sent to an output device, it must be translated into the proper form for humans. How this is actually done is beyond the scope of this discussion.

Representing Sounds

Sounds can be represented in the same binary scheme. A sound can be described by a set of three numbers representing its pitch, loudness and duration, and these numbers can be converted into the computer's binary code. Musical notes can also be represented as letters or pictures (notes on a staff), either of which can be represented with binary code.

SIMPLE PROCESSES

We have seen how computers represent various types of information, but computers do more than represent information, they also process it in various ways. It may seem surprising, but a few simple logical operations underlie all computer processes. Within computers, electronic devices called *logic gates* perform these operations. Each logic gate is a tiny processor that accepts one or two inputs and returns one output.

We represent the inputs and outputs as 0s and 1s. (If you are familiar with logical truth tables, think of 1 as *true* and 0 as *false*). Within the computer, the inputs and outputs are actually electrical signals.

All computer operations can be built from three types of simple logic gates, called NOT, OR and AND gates. Modern computers contain millions of logic gates, each microscopically tiny, on small pieces of silicon called *chips*. These amazing chips, the electronic workers of the computer age, can perform millions of logical operations each second.

The NOT logic gate takes a single input, either a 0 or a 1. The output is the other possible state. If a 1 goes in, a 0 comes out, if

INPUT   OUTPUT

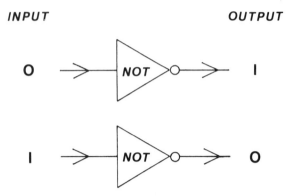

FIGURE A.2   The operation of the NOT gate. There is one input.
The output is 1 when the input 0. The output is 0 when the input
is 1.

a 0 goes in, a 1 comes out. That is, whatever goes in is NOT what
comes out. The operation of a NOT gate is shown in Figure A.2.

The OR logic gate requires two inputs. If either one OR the
other input is 1 (or both are 1), the output is 1; if both inputs are
0, the output is 0. The operation of an OR gate is shown in Figure
A.3.

INPUT   OUTPUT

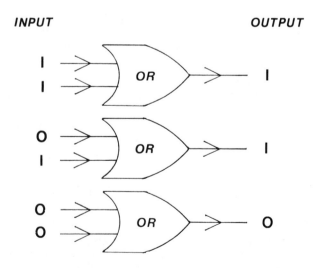

FIGURE A.3   The operation of the OR gate. There are two inputs.
The output is 1 when either or both inputs are 1. The output is 0
when both inputs are 0.

INPUT *OUTPUT*

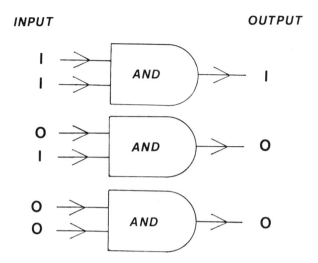

FIGURE A.4 The operation of the AND gate. There are two inputs. The output is 1 when both inputs are 1. The output is 0 when either or both inputs are 0.

The AND logic gate also takes two inputs. If both the first input AND the second input are 1, the output is 1; if one or both inputs are 0, the output is 0. The operation of an AND gate is shown in Figure A.4.

BUILDING MORE COMPLEX PROCESSES

Simple AND, OR and NOT operations are the fundamental building blocks of all computer processes. They are combined into slightly more complex processes, which are then recombined into even more complex processes, and so on through many levels. The key to understanding how computers work is to understand the simple processes and the principles for building more complex ones. In this section, I will describe how the progressive development of complex processes gets started.

As an example, I will describe how NOT, OR and AND logic gates can be combined to begin creating a comparison process. Comparison processes are important in many things computers do, such as determining whether two numbers are equal, two words match, or two pictures are identical. The example is somewhat detailed, but following it carefully will give you a good idea of how complex processes can be built from the simple logical operations.

Suppose, for example, we want the computer to compare two pictures such as the smiling and frowning faces earlier represented by dots of light in a 12 by 12 grid. These grids were coded in the computer as sequences of 1s and 0s, with 1 signifying a dot is lit and 0 signifying it is unlit. The computer could retrieve the binary representations of the two pictures and compare the corresponding points. Two points match if both are represented by 1 or both are represented by 0. If all the corresponding pairs of bits match, the two pictures are identical.

We want to build a device that will accept two inputs, give an output of 1 if the two inputs match and give an output of 0 if the two inputs do not match. We will call this a MATCH DETECTION device. Figure A.5 shows how it should work.

When both inputs are 1, The MATCH DETECTOR should give an output of 1. We already have a device which operates in this way—an AND gate. Therefore, an AND gate can serve as one part of the MATCH DETECTOR. We can rename the AND gate for its function and call it a TWO-1s DETECTOR.

We also need to detect when both inputs are 0. One way to do so is to combine two NOT gates with an AND gate, as shown in Figure A.6. The two bits to be compared are each used as an input to a NOT gate. The outputs from the two NOT gates then form the inputs to the AND gate. Try working through the diagram to

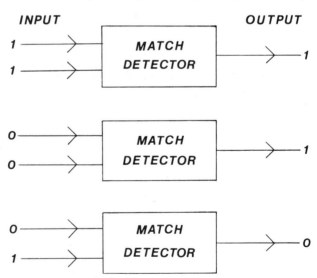

FIGURE A.5   How the MATCH DETECTOR should operate. There are two inputs. The output should be 1 when the inputs are both 1 or both 0. The output should be 0 when the inputs do not match.

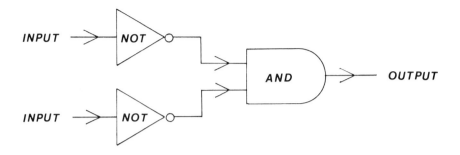

FIGURE A.6   TWO-0s DETECTOR. There are two inputs. The output is 1 when both inputs are 0. The output is 0 when one or both inputs are 1.

figure out what output this device will give for different inputs. If both input bits are 0, the output from each of the NOT gates would be 1. Since these form the input to AND, the output from AND would be 1. On the other hand, if one or both of the original bits are 1, the output from one or both of the NOT gates would be 0. Therefore the output from the AND gate would be 0. We can call this device a TWO-0s DETECTOR.

So far, we have two separate devices. One, consisting of a simple AND gate, has an output of 1 only if both inputs are 1. The other, a combination of two NOT gates and one AND gate, has an output of 1 only if both inputs are 0. Since we want our MATCH DETECTOR to accept either two 1s or two 0s as a match, we need to combine these two devices. This can be done with an OR gate, as shown in Figure A.7. The outputs of the TWO-1s DETECTOR and the TWO-0s DETECTOR serve as the input to the OR gate. If the output of either the TWO-0s DETECTOR or the TWO-1s DETECTOR is 1, then the final output from the MATCH DETECTOR will be 1. This tells us the two original bits match. If the outputs from both the TWO-0s DETECTOR and the TWO-1s DETECTOR are 0, the output from the MATCH DETECTOR will be 0. This tells us the two original bits do not match. This is exactly how we want our MATCH DETECTOR to operate.

The MATCH DETECTOR is just one part of a comparison process. To actually determine whether two pictures match, the computer would have to compare all the relevant bit-pairs and count the number of matches found. Therefore, the MATCH DETECTOR would have to be attached to a device that counts how many 1s and

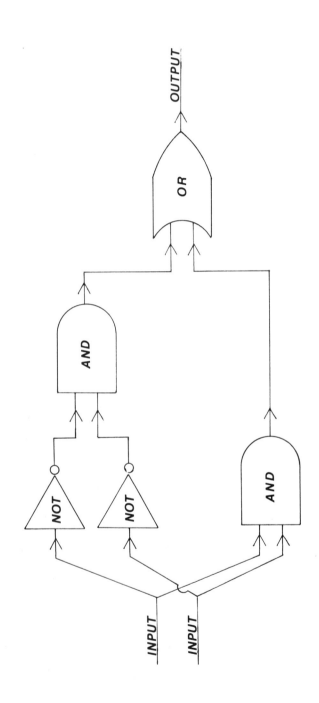

FIGURE A.7 The MATCH DETECTOR. There are two inputs. The output is 1 when the two inputs match and 0 when the two inputs do not match.

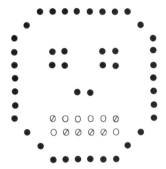

FIGURE A.8   The overlap of the smiling and frowning faces represented in a 12 by 12 grid.

● shows dots that appear in both faces.
⊘ shows dots that appear in the smiling face only.
○ shows dots that appear in the frowning face only.

0s are output. If the number of matches counted equals the number of bit-pairs compared, we would know that the two pictures are identical.

The MATCH DETECTOR provides a prototype of how all computer operations are built from simple ones. Try working through the diagram in figure A.7. Start with different inputs and see whether the final output is correct—1 if the inputs match, 0 if they do not. What would be the final state of the match counter after all the corresponding pairs of bits from the smiling and frowning faces were compared? The two faces are identical except for the mouths. Figure A.8 shows the overlap of the faces. The filled dots are in both faces, the dots with the slash inside are in the smile face only, and the empty dots are in the frowning face only. The face pictures are represented in a 12 by 12 grid, so there are 144 pairs of bits to be compared. As you can see, the faces differ in twelve dot positions. Therefore, the match counter would find 132 matching bit-pairs and 12 mismatching bit-pairs.

Once the MATCH DETECTOR is created it can be used as a building block in more complex processes. Since it operates upon binary symbols, it can be applied to the computer's representations of numbers, words, pictures or sounds. It can be part of a process to determine whether two numbers are equal, two words are the same, two pictures are identical or two sounds match. Building more complex processes from simpler ones, and then using the new processes to create even more sophisticated ones, eventually leads to everything computers can do.

MACHINE LANGUAGE AND ASSEMBLY LANGUAGE

At this point, it may seem inordinately difficult to program a computer do anything interesting, since the entire process has to be built from simple logical operations. However, computer programmers do not actually work at the level of NOT, AND and OR gates. When a computer is designed, the simple logical operations are used to build a set of *machine language instructions* into the central processing unit (CPU). These are commands the CPU is built to follow. They constitute what can be thought of as the computer's native language.

Each machine language instruction may trigger the coordinated action of many simple operations. Machine language provides the programmer with instructions to tell the computer to add or subtract, move information into or out of memory, compare bits (like our MATCH DETECTOR), jump from one part of the program to another, and perform a variety of other functions. The programmer working with machine language only needs to be concerned with the function of each of these instructions. He does not need to know how it is carried out by the logic gates within the CPU.

Programming in machine language, while preferable to using the simple logical operations directly, is still difficult and tedious. Machine language is more compatible with the electronic logic of computers than with the ways people think. Table A.3 shows part of a machine language program as a programmer would enter it

TABLE A.3
Part of a Machine Language Prrogram

033A 20	35	FD
033D 8D	01	60
0340 20	35	FD
0343 DD	01	60
0346 D0	05	
0348 A9	59	
034A 4C	01	
034C A9	49	
034E 8D	00	04
0351 4D	3A	03

into a computer. Looking at the program will not give you any clue about what it instructs the computer to do, as the programmer has to use the computer's internal codes for instructions. Programming in machine language is akin to communicating in Morse Code. Both are designed to fit machines, not people. While people can use machine language or Morse code, in either case it is slow, tedious, and error-prone work.

Machine language has a close relative, called *assembly language*, which is somewhat easier for people to use. In assembly language, mnemonic letter codes are used for instructions and programming is made easier in a number of other ways. A program called an *assembler* automatically translates assembly language into machine language for the computer. A sample piece of an assembly language program is shown in Table A.4. It is still not obvious from looking at the program what it tells the computer to do, but the assembly language instructions at least provide some hints. For example, the last line of the program tells the computer to jump (JMP) back to the first instruction, which has been labeled START.

Assembly language is used by some programmers for certain types of programs. It lets them use all the capabilities of the computer and make their programs operate more quickly than with any other language except machine language. However, assembly language is a direct translation of machine language, and therefore it also reflects the nature of computers more than the ways people think.

To make their work easier, programmers most often use *high level languages* that are much more like human languages. Translation programs, technically called *interpreters* and *compilers*, translate high level languages into machine language. High level languages are discussed in Chapter 9.

TABLE A.4
Part of an Assembly Language Program

```
START    JSR  CHARGET
         STA  6001
         JSR  CHARGET
         CMP  6001
         BNE  NOMATCH
         LDA  84
         JMP  DISPLAY
NOMATCH  LDA  68
DISPLAY  STA  4000
         JMP  START
```

Appendix B

Chapter Notes and Sources of Further Information

My aim in describing the example programs and devices in Chapters 1 through 10 was to demonstrate the myriad possible uses of computers in education. In many cases I described specific existing products. The companies that produce these products are listed in the following chapter notes. When no company is listed for an example program, the description was based either upon very common types of programs (e.g., Logo, word processing) or upon a synthesis of features found in existing programs, current research and development, programs available on large computers (most often Control Data Corporation's Plato system) and my own ideas. All of the programs described are feasible with current personal computers, and new and better educational software is rapidly becoming available.

The notes for each chapter also include suggested readings that provide more information about the topics covered in the chapter. Many of the suggested readings contain information about specific software and hardware products.

I have tried to select the most useful and readily available references, and to provide as current a list as possible. However, things change very quickly in the world of computers. To help you find up-to-date information, the notes for Chapter 11 list periodicals, information directories and sources of software reviews and catalogs.

The final section of this appendix contains the addresses of companies whose products are described and publishers of the periodicals, catalogs and directories listed.

CHAPTER 1 NOTES

Oregon Trail is available from the Minnesota Educational Computing Consortium (MECC).

The Pinball Construction Set is available from Electronic Arts.

Maxit is available from Cursor Magazine.

Square Pairs is available from Scholastic, Inc.

An electronic mail service is provided by the Source, as well as other companies.

Large information bases are provided by Dialog, the Source, and other companies.

The spelling drill program is available from Teaching Tools: Microcomputer Services.

The function plotter program is available from J.L. Hammett.

See the Chapter 10 notes for information about special programs and devices for handicapped individuals.

Suggested Readings:

Deken, J. *The Electronic Cottage.* New York: Willam Morrow and Company, 1982.

Papert, S. *Mindstorms: Children, Computers and Powerful Ideas.* New York: Basic Books, 1980.

Peterson, D., ed. *The Intelligent Schoolhouse: Readings on Computers and Learning.* Reston, VA: Reston Publishing, 1984.

Taylor, R.P., ed. *The Computer in the School: Tutor, Tool, Tutee.* New York: Teachers College Press, 1980.

Toffler, A. *The Third Wave.* New York: Willam Morrow and Company, 1979.

Wilkinson, A.C.,ed. *Classroom Computers and Cognitive Science.* New York: Academic Press, 1983.

CHAPTER 2 NOTES

Suggested Readings:

Barger, R.N. "The Computer as a Humanizing Influence in Education," *T.H.E. Journal* 10, May 1983, pp. 109-111.

Capron, H.L. & Williams, B.K. *Computers and Data Processing*. Menlo Park, CA: Benjamin/Cummings, 1982.

Covvey, H.D. & McAlister, N.H. *Computer Consciousness*. Reading, MA: Addison-Wesley, 1980.

Editors of Consumers Guide. *Illustrated Computer Dictionary*. New York: Exeter Books, 1983.

Evans, C. *The Micro Millenium*. New York: Washington Square Press, 1979.

Garetz, M. *Bits, Bytes and Buzzwords*. Beverton, OR: Dilithium Press, 1983.

Laurie, P. *The Micro Revolution*. New York: Universe Books, 1981.

McWilliams, P.A. *The Personal Computer Book*. Los Angeles: Prelude Press, 1982.

Mansfield, R., Miller, M.D., Martinek, K.E., and Lock, R. *The Beginner's Guide to Buying a Personal Computer*. Greensboro, NC: Compute! Books, 1982.

Moody, R. *The First Book of Microcomputers*. Rochelle Park, NJ: Hayden Book Company, 1978.

Weizenbaum, J. *Computer Power and Human Reason*. San Francisco: W.H. Freeman, 1976.

CHAPTER 3 NOTES

The *Bank Street Writer* program is available from Broderbund Software (home version) and Scholastic, Inc. (school version). Many other word processing programs are available.

The graphics creation program that uses a joystick is a combination of *Paint* (available from Reston Publishing Company) and *Edu-Paint* (available from SOFTSWAP). The graphics creation program that uses the graphics tablet is the *Designer's Toolkit*, available from Apple Computer. Many other graphics creation programs are available.

Suggested Readings:

Greenberg, D., Marcus, A., Schmidt, A.H., & Gorter, V. *The Computer Image: Applications of Computer Graphics*. Reading, MA: Addison-Wesley, 1982.

Grossberger, L. & Vertelney, H. "The Art Machine," *Educational Computer*, Jan/Feb 1983, pp. 12-14.

Halfhill, T. "Selecting the Right Word Processor," *Compute*, April 1983, pp. 24-31.

Holder, W. "Software Tools for Writers," *Byte*, July 1982, pp. 138-163.

Kleiman, G.M. "Computers in the Art Class," *Compute!*, November, 1982.

McWilliams, P.A. *The Word Processing Book*. Los Angeles: Prelude Press, 1982.

Mercuri, R.T. "Music Editors for Small Computers," *Creative Computing*, February 1981, pp. 18-24.

Myers, R.E. *Microcomputer Graphics*. Reading, MA: Addison-Wesley, 1982.

Pelczarski, M. & Tate, J. (eds.). *The Creative Apple*. Morris Plains, NJ: Creative Computing Press, 1982.

Press, L. *Low-Cost Word Processing*. Reading, MA: Addison-Wesley, 1983.

Steele, D.J. & Wills, B.L. "Microcomputer-Assisted Instruction for Musical Performance Skills," *T.H.E. Journal*, January 1982, pp. 58-60.

Thornburg, T. *Picture This!*. Reading, MA: Addison-Wesley, 1982.

See also the readings on Logo and turtle graphics listed in the Chapter 9 notes.

CHAPTER 4 NOTES

Dialog is available from Dialog Information Retrieval Service.

VisiCalc is a trademark of Personal Software, Inc., VisiCorp.

Information and electronic mail services are available from the Source Telecomputing Corporation.

Suggested Readings:

Beil, D.H. *The VisiCalc®Book*. Reston, VA: Reston Publishing Company, 1983.

Castlewitz, D.M. & Chisausky, L.J. *VisiCalc®Home and Office Companion*. Berkeley, CA: Osborn/McGraw-Hill, 1982.

Glossbrenner, A. *Personal Computer Communications*. New York: St. Martin's Press, 1983.

Kruginsky, D. *DataBase Management Systems: A Guide to Micro-computer Software*. Berkeley, CA: Osborne/McGraw Hill, 1983.

Simundi, T. *What If?: A Guide to Computer Modeling*. Los Angeles: The Book Company, 1983.

CHAPTER 5 NOTES

Roadtrip is available from SOFTSWAP.

Oregon Trail is available from Minnesota Educational Computing Consortium (MECC).

Suggested Readings:

Ahl, D.H. (ed). *Computers in Science and Social Studies: A Sourcebook of Ideas*. Morris Plains, NJ: Creative Computing Press, 1983.

Roberts, N., Andersen, D., Deal, R., Garet, M., and Shaffer, W. *Introduction to Computer Simulation: A System Dynamics Modeling Approach*. Reading, MA: Addison-Wesley, 1983.

CHAPTER 6 NOTES

The *Adventure Game* described is based in part on one available from Adventure International. Many other companies also market Adventure Game programs.

Facemaker is available from Spinnaker Software.

Pinball Construction Set is available from Electronic Arts.

Crossword Magic is available from L & S Computerware.

Raise the Flags is available from Apple Computer.

Darts is available from Apple Computer (as part of the *Elementary My Dear Apple* package).

Coordinate Monsters is based in part upon *Green Globs* (available from Conduit) and *Carroll Critters* (available from Wadsworth Electronic Publishing).

Maxit is available from Cursor magazine.

What's Next? is based in part upon *Moptown* from The Learning Company.

Square Pairs is available from Scholastic, Inc.

Suggested Readings:

Ahl, D. "Learning Can be Fun," *Creative Computing*, April 1983, pp. 98-143.

Dugdale, S. "There's a Green Glob in Your Classroom," *Classroom Computer News*. March 1983, pp. 40-43.

Goles, G.G. "Games as Teaching Tools," *Educational Computer*, Nov/Dec 1982, pp. 12-15 and Jan/Feb 1983, pp. 41-44.

Malone, T. "What Makes Computer Games Fun?" *Byte*, December, 1981, pp. 258-282.

CHAPTER 7 NOTES
Suggested Readings:

Ahl, D.H. *Computers in Science and Social Studies: A Sourcebook of Ideas*. Morris Plains, NJ: Creative Computing Press, 1983.

Geoffrion, L.D. & Geoffrion, O.P. *Computers and Reading Instruction*. Reading, MA: Addison-Wesley, 1983.

Godfrey, D. & Sterling, S. *The Elements of CAL: The How-To Book of Computer Aided Learning*. Reston, VA: Reston Publishing Co., 1982.

Kelman, P., Bardige, A., Choate, J., Hanify, G., Richards, J., Roberts, N., Walters, J., & Tornrose, M.K. *Computers in Teaching Mathematics*. Reading, MA: Addison-Wesley, 1983.

Kleiman, G.M. & Humphrey, M. "Writing Your Own Software with Authoring Tools," *Electronic Learning*, May/June 1982, pp. 37-41.

Mason, G.E., Blanchard, J.S. & Daniel, D.B. *Computer Applications in Reading*. Newark, DE: International Reading Association, 1983.

CHAPTER 8 NOTES

Mastertype is available from Lightning Software.

Meteor Multiplication is available from Developmental Learning Materials.

The addition and spelling drill examples are based on programs developed by Teaching Tools: Microcomputer Services.

The music drill examples are based on programs available from Minnesota Educational Computing Consortium (MECC).

Suggested Readings:

Kleiman, G.M., Humphrey, M. & Lindsay, P.H. "Microcomputers and Hyperactive Children." *Creative Computing*, March 1981, pp. 93-94.

Lambrecht, J.J. & Pullis, J.M. "Computer Assisted Instruction in Typing," *Educational Computer*, May/June 1983, pp. 42-45;66-68.

See also the suggested readings for Chapter 7.

CHAPTER 9 NOTES

Suggested Readings:

Abelson, H. *Logo for the Apple II*. Peterborough, NH: Byte/McGraw Hill, 1982.

Brown, P. *Pascal from BASIC*. Reading, MA: Addison-Wesley, 1982.

Dwyer, T. & Critchfield. *BASIC and the Personal Computer*. Reading, MA: Addison-Wesley, 1978.

Dwyer, T. & Critchfield. *A Bit of BASIC*. Reading, MA: Addison-Wesley, 1980.

Kleiman, G.M. "Gentle Introductions to Programming," *Compute!*, January 1983.

Pattis, R.E. *Karel the Robot: A Gentle Introduction to the Art of Programming*. New York: John Wiley & Sons, 1981.

Special Issue on Logo. *Byte*, August 1982.

Thornburg, D. "Friends of the Turtle." Monthly column in *Compute* magazine.

Watt, D. *Learning with Logo*. New York: McGraw-Hill, 1983.

CHAPTER 10 NOTES

The description of the development of special devices and programs for Jane is based upon work at the Ontario Crippled Children's Center, Stanford Children's Hospital, and other special centers for the handicapped.

The Express 3 Communications Device is available from Prentke-Romich Company.

Speech synthesizers for personal computers are made by Votrax, Street Electronics, and other companies.

The *Optacon* and *VersaBraille* are available from Telesensory.

Kurzweil Reading Machine is available from Kurzweil Computer Products, Inc.

Special Keyboards are made by Prentke-Romich and other companies.

Speech recognition devices for personal computers are made by Scott Instruments, Voicetek, and other companies.

For more information about available computer aids for handicapped individuals, see: Vanderheiden, G.C. & Walstead, L.M. *International Software/Hardware Registry* (available from the Trace Research and Development Center).

Suggested Readings:

Goldenberg, E.P. *Special Technology for Special Children.* Baltimore: University Park Press, 1979.

Goldenberg, E.P., Carter, C.J., Russell, S.J., Stokes, S. & Sylvester, M.J. *Computers, Education and Special Needs.* Reading, MA: Addison-Wesley, 1983.

IEEE Computer Society. *Proceedings of the Johns Hopkins First National Search for Applications of Personal Computing to Aid the Handicapped.* Los Angeles: IEEE Computer Society, 1981.

Vanderheiden, G.C. "Computers Can Play a Dual Role for Disabled Individuals," *Byte*, September 1982, pp. 136-162.

CHAPTER 11 NOTES

Suggested Books:

Coborn, P., Kelman, P., Roberts, N., Snyder, T.F.F., Watt, D.H. & Weiner, C. *Practical Guide to Computers in Education.* Reading, MA: Addison-Wesley, 1982.

Lathrop, A. & Goodson, B. *Courseware in the Classroom.* Reading, MA: Addison-Wesley, 1983.

See also the suggested readings for Chapters 1 and 2.

Monthly columns on Computers and Education:

Kleiman, G.M. "Learning with Computers," *Compute!*.

Watt, D. "Educational Computing," *Popular Computing*.

Varven, J. "Schoolhouse Apple," *Softalk*.

Periodicals Focusing on Computers and Education:

Classroom Computer Learning
The Computing Teacher
Educational Computer
Educational Technology
Electronic Education
Electronic Learning
Teaching and Computers
T.H.E. Journal

General Computer Periodicals That Include Articles on Education:

Byte
Compute!
Creative Computing
Personal Computing
Popular Computing

Directories of Information (Updated Annually):

Classroom Computer Learning Directory of Educational Computing Resources.

Instructor Magazine Computer Directory for Schools.

Software Reviews and Catalogs of Selected Educational Software:

Courseware Report Card (software reviews)
Follett Library Book Company educational software catalog
J.L. Hammett educational software catalog
K-12 MicroMedia educational software catalog
Opportunities for Learning educational software catalog
Scholastic, Inc. educational software catalog

ADDRESS LIST

Adventure International, Box 3435, Longwood, FL 32750.

Apple Computer, Inc., 20525 Mariani Ave, Cupertino, CA 95014.

Broderbund Software, Inc., 1938 Fourth St., San Rafael, CA 94901.

Byte Magazine, 70 Main St., Peterborough, NH 03458.

Classroom Computer Learning Magazine and Directory, 19 Davis Ave., Belmont, CA 94002.

Compute! Magazine, Small Systems Services, P.O. Box 5406, Greensboro, NC 27403.

The Computing Teacher, Dept. of Computer and Information Science, University of Oregon, Eugene, OR 97403.

Conduit, P.O. Box 388, Iowa City, IA 52244.

Courseware Report Card, 150 West Carob Street, Compton, CA 90220.

Creative Computing Magazine, P.O. Box 789-M, Morristown, NJ 07960.

Cursor Magazine, The Code Works, Box 550, Goleta, CA 93116.

Developmental Learning Materials, #1 DLM Park, Allen, TX 75002.

Dialog Information Services, Inc., 3460 Hillview Ave, Palo Alto, CA 94304.

Educational Computer Magazine, 10439 N. Stelling Road, Cupertino, CA 95014.

Educational Technology Magazine, 140 Sylvan Ave, Englewood Cliffs, NJ 07632.

Electronic Arts, 2755 Campus Drive, San Mateo, CA 94403.

Electronic Education Magazine, 1311 Executive Center Drive, Tallahassee, FL 32301.

Electronic Learning Magazine, Scholastic, Inc., 902 Sylvan Ave, Englewood Cliffs, NJ 07632.

Follett Library Book Company, 4506 Northwest Highway, Crystal Lake, IL 60014.

J.L. Hammett Co. Hammett Place, Box 545, Braintree, MA 02184.

Instructor Magazine and Directory, 757 Third Ave, New York, NY 10017.

K-12 MicroMedia, P.O. Box 17, Valley Cottage, NY 10989.

Kurzweil Computer Products, Inc., 33 Cambridge Parkway, Cambridge, MA 02142.

L & S Computerware, 1589 Fraser Drive, Sunnyvale, CA 94087.

The Learning Company, 545 Middlefield Road, Menlo Park, CA 94025.

Lightning Software, P.O. Box 11725, Palo Alto, CA 94306.

Minnesota Educational Computing Consortium (MECC), 2520 Broadway Drive, St. Paul, MN 55113.

Opportunities for Learning, 8950 Lurline Ave., Chatsworth, CA 91311.

Personal Computing Magazine, P.O. Box 1408, Riverton, NJ 08077.

Popular Computing Magazine, 70 Main Street, Peterborough, NH 03458.

Prentke-Romich Company, R.D. 2, Box 191, Shreve, OH 44676.

Reston Publishing Company, 11480 Sunset Hills Road, Reston, VA 22090.

Scholastic, Inc., 2931 East McCarty Street, Jefferson City, MO 65102.

Scott Instruments, 1111 Willow Springs Drive, Denton, TX 76201.

Softalk Magazine, 11021 Magnolia Blvd, N. Hollywood, CA 91601.

Softswap, San Mateo County Office of Education, 333 Main Street, Redwood City, CA 94063.

Source Telecomputing Corp., 1616 Anderson Road, McLean, VA 22102.

Spinnaker Software Corp., 215 First Street, Cambridge, MA 02142.

Street Electronics, 1140 Mark Ave, Carpinteria, CA 93013.

Teaching and Computers Magazine. Scholastic, Inc., 902 Sylvan Ave, Englewood Cliffs, NJ 07632.

Teaching Tools: Microcomputer Services, P.O. Box 50065, Palo Alto, CA 94303.

Telesensory Systems, Inc., 3408 Hillview Ave, P.O. Box 10099, Palo Alto, CA 94304.

Trace Research and Development Center for the Severely Communicatively Handicapped, University of Wisconsin, WI 53706.

VisiCorp, 2895 Zanker Road, San Jose, CA 95134.

Voicetek, P.O. Box 388, Goleta, CA 93116.

Votrax, 500 Stephenson Highway, Troy, MI 48084.

Wadsworth Electronic Publishing, Statler Office Bldg #1435, Boston, MA 02116.

Index